# FOUR SEASONS OF
# ORCHIDS

# FOUR SEASONS OF
# ORCHIDS

GREG ALLIKAS & NED NASH

CREATIVE
HOMEOWNER®

First Published in the United States of America in 2007 by

# CRE▲TIVE
## HOMEOWNER®

Creative Homeowner® is a registered trademark of
Federal Marketing Corporation

Produced by Salamander Books
An imprint of Anova Books Company Ltd
10 Southcombe Street, London W14 0RA

Printed and bound by
Craftprint International Ltd, Singapore

Current printing (last digit): 12 11 10 9 8 7 6 5 4 3 2 1
Library of Congress card number: 2007921258
ISBN 10: 1-58011-351-6
ISBN 13: 978-1-58011-351-9

CREATIVE HOMEOWNER
A Division of Federal Marketing Corp.
24 Park Way
Upper Saddle River, NJ 07458
www.creativehomeowner.com

CREDITS
**Editor:** Frank Hopkinson
**Consultant:** Greg Allikas and Ned Nash
**Designer:** John Heritage
**Indexer:** Colin Hynson
**Production:** Kate Rogers
**Color Reproduction:** Anorax Imaging

Picture credits

Cover images © Greg Allikas
All other images © Greg Allikas with the exception of page 59
(right) which was taken by Neil Sutherland

Additional captions

**Page 1:** *Dendrobium amethystoglossum*
**Page 2:** *Laeliocattleya* Gold Digger 'Orglade's
Mandarin'
**Page 3:** *Angulocaste* Santa Barbara
**Page 5:** *Epilaeliocattleya* Rojorufa

# CONTENTS

# INTRODUCTION

*Orchids were once collected and admired by society's elite. Today, with the explosion of hybridization and new cultural techniques, anyone can acquire a dazzling collection.*

The world is full of orchid-related myths. They're difficult to grow. They're expensive. The flowers are short-lived. They are never fragrant. *There is only one orchid season.* Throughout this book, we will be dealing with, and discounting, myths about orchids. However, the myth that dissuades many plant lovers is that one simply cannot have orchid flowers year round, at least not without some costly and complicated techniques unavailable to the everyday grower.

The truth is, with some planning; a little space in your home, greenhouse, or on your patio, and a dozen or so well-chosen plants, you can dispel this particular myth for yourself by having orchids in flower all year long. Modern cultural techniques also allow a broad selection of blooming orchids to be available throughout the year for your last-minute decorating needs. Many people buy orchids one or two at a time, in flower or in bud to bloom soon, every month or six weeks, as a way of building a small collection with a diverse and complete annual blooming cycle.

On the way to discovering how you can have orchids in bloom for all four seasons of the year, you will learn that some orchids are indeed rather difficult for the inexperienced grower to manage. At the same time you will find illustrations and descriptions of many other easily accessible plants that are no more trouble—and in many cases, considerably less trouble—than the average house or garden plant.

**Left:** *Cattleya* 'Wendy Patterson' has an elegant, pure white flower.

**Right:** Although a challenging subject for some growers, the beautifully veined lip of *Cattleya dowiana* has made it a favorite *Cattleya* species.

Some of the most expensive plants ever sold have been orchids. These are the exception though, and today, more than ever, good quality orchids in vast array are readily available to even the least green-fingered buyer.

There is an orchid revolution underway that is unprecedented in the history of horticulture, driven in large part by the great value represented by flowering orchid plants. Orchids are a great value simply because the floral display is much longer lasting than a comparably priced floral arrangement or potted flowering plant. Orchid flowers can be incredibly long-lived, even in less-than-favorable home conditions, with their flower life sometimes measured not in days or weeks, but months.

Flowering plants use fragrance to attract pollinators. Scent is a much more powerful attractant than sight in many cases and is effective over a much greater distance. Orchids are no different in their use of fragrance, except perhaps in degree, possessing some of the most penetrating of all perfumes, whether sweet or spicy, pleasing or putrid, delicate or piercing. Many produce their scents only at certain times of day or night, when their pollinators are most active in nature. Entire orchid collections can be, and have been, based on fragrance alone.

Taken as a whole—long-lasting flowers in a vast array of colors and patterns, blooms throughout the year, and attractive perfumes—it is easy to see why orchids have vaulted into the forefront of modern horticulture. While orchids have not always enjoyed the wide general popularity that they do today, theirs is a rich and storied history, full of tradition and folklore. The traditional orchid

**Below:** *Phalaenopsis* 'Balden's Kaleidoscope' is a good example of the moth orchid and easily grown and maintained.

**Right:** *Aerides odorata* is a good example of an epiphytic orchid. Profuse aerial roots take up moisture and nutrients for this Asian tree dweller.

enthusiast, as opposed to the more casual modern day hobbyist, was often quite a character, full of passion and quirky obsession. In many cases, people interested in growing orchids had to go to extraordinary lengths to satisfy their hobby. Deceit and outright theft were not unheard of.

Today's grower can enjoy these sometimes outlandish stories while reaping the benefit of over 200 years of horticultural experience with an abundance of reasonably priced, beautiful orchid flowers in variety never previously imagined.

Our goal in this book is to remove, or at least reduce, some of the anxiety that is inevitably associated with one's early orchid purchases. The best known cure for fear and anxiety, of course, is knowledge. How we arrived where we are today in orchids is a subject that increasingly few are qualified to convey. The history, biology, simple taxonomy—why *do* they have those names?—and proven cultural methods will all be explained in a way that is easy to understand and simple to practice. What's more, this comprehensive, though necessarily concise, seasonal guide to orchids will not only enhance the novice's pleasure in the

hobby, but will be of more than passing interest to the more experienced grower.

Not only will we illustrate the very best of today's top orchids, we will offer purchasing tips on how to obtain just the type of orchid you have in mind. The variety of orchids now available is to a large extent made possible by advances in cultural techniques that allow growers to save a great deal of time in the production of flowering size plants. Unfortunately, these same techniques can also make the plants more difficult to acclimate to less-than-ideal (as in the typical home or garden) circumstances. We'll find out why and disclose the methods you can use to greatly increase your chances of success with these plants.

You will also see how to find sources that are not so readily available, where the plants will be distinct from the more commonly marketed varieties, and where you will be more likely to find plants grown by "old school" orchid professionals. These professionals are one of the often overlooked sources of local knowledge that will enhance your cultural endeavors.

No single horticultural book will have all the answers. We urge you to read and study widely. But start here!

# THE HISTORY OF ORCHIDS

*The history of orchid cultivation has been one of trial and multiple error as orchid hunters and nurserymen have sought to replicate their native habitats in less advantageous conditions.*

The Chinese provide the earliest written record of orchids. Circa 2800 BC the terrestrial *Bletilla hyacinthina* was described as part of a herbal remedy. Confucius, around 500 BC, used the term "lan" and described his subject as the "king of fragrance." This orchid was almost certainly *Cymbidium ensifolium*, still grown and prized in Asian culture for its delicate foliage and heavenly perfume. Of the many cultivars still grown today, aberrant foliar or floral characters distinguish the

most venerated and valuable. Here in the West, *Cym. ensifolium* is prized more for its contribution to heat-tolerant hybrids than for its intrinsic appeal. Chinese orchid culture has, as with so much else, the longest continuous active history. This love of orchids is unabated today.

### Japanese influence

The Japanese most certainly inherited their love of orchids from the Chinese. Orchids have played an important part in traditional Japanese culture where they are appreciated for their serenity and beauty as well as their symbolic representation of royalty and elegance.

There are two native Japanese orchids in particular that have both a significant place in Japanese culture, as well as a highly visible modern relevance. *Dendrobium moniliforme* has been important in Japanese royal collections for hundreds of years, and today distinctive cultivars are highly sought after. Such rare and valuable plants are only occasionally exhibited and attract considerable attention from the public—not only for their multitude of foliar and floral differences, but as symbols of wealth and privilege.

The Samurai class was passionate about *Neofinetia falcata*, the wind orchid, which they collected for the diminutive fan-shaped foliage and the purest white, sweetly scented, bird-like blooms. Japanese history is rife with tales

**Left:** *Bletilla striata* (syn. *Bletilla hyacinthina*) is one of the earliest recorded orchid species. Today it is often grown as a landscape plant in areas with mild winters.

**Right:** The fragrant *Cymbidium ensifolium* is believed to have been admired by the great Chinese philosopher Confucius.

Left: Japanese Samurai warriors would take the orchid *Neofinetia falcata* with them into battle.

of Samurai carrying their plants of *Neo. falcata* into battle to enjoy a moment of serenity between skirmishes.

Today, distinctive forms of *Neo. falcata*, as with *Den. moniliforme*, are still symbolic of Japan's rich past and are prized, not only by wealthy and fanatic Japanese growers, but by Western aficionados as well. The finest cultivars of either of these orchids can fetch prices well into the thousands, and occasionally, tens of thousands of dollars.

## Orchids in the West

The Asiatic history of orchids stretches much further back than Western orchid history. However, as in Asian history, the first mention of orchids comes as part of an herbal remedy. Theophrastus, the "Father of Botany" and pupil of Plato and Aristotle, first wrote of orchids in his *Enquiry Into Plants* around 300 BC. He coined the name "orchis" in reference to the testicle-like appearance of the orchid's underground tubers.

Later, Dioscorides writes about orchids in his *Materia Medica* of around AD 70. During this period, Western medicine and herbal remedies were based on the Doctrine of Signatures, the basic tenet of which was that naturally

occurring organisms, or portions of organisms, that resembled a part of the human anatomy were effective in curing disease associated with the portion of the anatomy they most resembled. Therefore, the testicle-like tubers of orchis and other Eurasian terrestrial orchids were thought to influence male virility, i.e. an early form of Viagra.

## Contemporary History

The contemporary history of orchids begins in the early eighteenth century. The scientific and entrepreneurial thirst for new materials of potentially great economic value, coupled with the aristocracy's hunger for novelty, sent plant collectors on a quest through both the New and Old World for ever-newer and more distinct plants and animals.

As the tropics began to divulge their wonders to explorers, new plants and animals began to flood back to Europe. These new plants and animals needed names that would help to identify them as distinct and different from other, similar organisms. Identification required close investigation using the developing scientific method. Much of this flurry of discovery predates Linnaeus and his binomial system, so plants and animals were named,

**Above:** A specimen of *Bletia verecunda* was returned to England to be dried and mounted, but when its new owner noted signs of life, it was potted up and subsequently bloomed.

seemingly randomly, according to their attributes and in a descriptive way.

The most important aspect of the process was the storage and cataloging of items so that once categorized they could be referenced and compared with other, newer organisms. The first tropical orchid entered cultivation in England in 1731 as a "dried" herbarium specimen, ready for cataloging and storage. The recipient, a horticulturist as well as a scientist, noted some life still in the plant, and potted it up. It subsequently grew and flowered. The descriptive, non-Linnaean name given this new species was *Helleborine virginianum flore rotundo luteo.* This plant, later named *Bletia verecunda,* was the vanguard of many millions of plants to follow.

### The first Cattleya

The discovery of a showy new orchid, or a locale with several new plants, often had such great potential economic value that the explorers would not disclose the exact location. In many cases, they may not have even known the precise location, as this was long before modern mapping techniques. Every plant and animal evidencing even the slightest potential interest was quickly sent back to Europe. So, if the desirable item was not the object of original interest, its collection location was probably not noted. The most famous example of this problem concerned one of the premier orchids of all time, *Cattleya labiata.* The first plants of this species arrived in England in the early nineteenth century as packing material around other plants thought to be of higher interest and value.

The shipment originated in the Organ Mountains around Rio de Janeiro, Brazil. The recipient was William Cattley of Barnet in England, a noted patron of horticulture and seminal orchid hobbyist, who found more interest in the packing material than in the packed plants, and attempted the cultivation of these strange new objects. Amazingly, later that same year, in November 1818, a plant flowered, and it was stunning, quite unlike any flower seen to date. John Lindley, another key player in the golden age of orchids, christened the new plant after its cultivator, as *Cattleya labiata autumnalis* (autumn-flowering, large-lipped cattleya.)

The exact location of the plants' collection had not been recorded and the plants were a much-treasured rarity for a period of nearly 20 years before it was relocated and more plants could be imported. In 1836, a Dr. Gardner rediscovered the species and recorded its habitat in his journal. Commercial collectors flocked there, decimating the habitat to provide plants for a demanding clientele in the homeland, creating a pattern that would be seen again and again, up until the present day.

It was William Spencer Cavendish, sixth Duke of Devonshire, who can be credited with starting the love of orchid collecting among British aristocrats. In 1833, Messrs. Loddiges, pioneers in early orchid growing, displayed at a Royal Horticultural Society exhibition in London, a plant of the butterfly orchid (*Oncidium papilio*), now known as *Psychopsis Papilio.* At this time, most epiphytic orchids were known as Epidendrums or Air Plants. Lord Cavendish was so taken with this stunning new plant that he immediately bought it. This was the beginning of one of the great amateur orchid collections.

As Cavendish began to exhibit orchids, both at his estate and at the regular exhibitions at the Royal

Horticultural Society, orchid collecting quickly became the "thing to do" among the wealthy and landed rich. Other important early hobbyists included Hugh Cuming, Skinner and Bowring, Harrison and Moss, Cattley, Rucker, and Day, all of whom are immortalized in orchid history by eponymous names such as the genus *Cattleya* and species such as *Cattleya skinneri*, *Lycaste skinneri*, *C. bowringiana*, *C. harrisoniana*, *Bifrenaria harrisoniae*, *Anguloa ruckeri*, and *Coelogyne dayana*.

## Orchid Adventurers

As new locales were explored, new plants were sent back by commercial collectors. They were also grown in tropical plant nurseries as well as fledgling orchid nurseries. Getting orchids home intact was an enormously difficult business. Even today, importing orchids from another country, even from an established nursery, is fraught with headaches and heartaches. One hundred or more years ago, orchids collected from the wild would be taken to a port by donkey to be loaded onto a sailing ship or, in later days, a steamship to travel the many days and weeks back to a European port where they would be sold at auction.

**Above:** The very first cattleya, *Cattleya labiata*, was originally sent over as packing material for what plant hunters had regarded as more interesting plant specimens.

The losses in transit were enormous—plants would either dehydrate from exposure or rot from being crowded together in tight packing crates. The literature is also rife with stories of collectors who perished in the line of duty.

We cannot help but admire the men who faced unknown geography, new insects, foul diseases, and often hostile natives on their way to finding the orchids they sought. As noted with *C. labiata*, the collectors were not shy in the quantity of plants they stripped from the habitat. The wholesale collection methods were designed not only to meet demand and hedge against losses in transit, but in the knowledge that if an area were completely depleted of a given species, it would be impossible for competitors to affect the market. All too often, the trees in which they grew would be cut down, not just to make the collection easier, but also to ruin the habitat for any survivors. Huge numbers of plants were sent off to European markets, measured by the crate or by the ton. Contemporary journals tell of shipments of 10,000 *Odontoglossum crispum* which resulted in their being "extinguished in this spot."

## The Father of Orchidology

The leading botanists of the day anxiously awaited the new plants' flowering so that the discoveries might be recorded by painting or drawing, officially described and named. Systematic botany began to come into its own. Naturally, each family or genus had its hero, and the preeminent orchid hero was John Lindley, often called the "Father of Modern Orchidology."

Although Lindley worked in other plant groups as well, his contributions to the study and classification of orchids are his main source of lasting fame. He is credited with the coining of the family name, Orchidaceae, from the earlier *Orchideae de Jussieu* in his book *The Genera and Species of Orchidaceous Plants*. Perhaps his most significant work

---

**Below:** The orchid hunter George Ure Skinner was said to have crossed the Atlantic 39 times in his pursuit of exotic orchids. His reward was the eponymous *Cattleya skinneri*

is *Folia Orchidaceae*, the goal of which was to be a monographic treatment of all orchid genera and was unfortunately never completed. However, certainly more significant to orchid growers today were his suggestions, based on habitat knowledge, to Joseph Paxton on how to successfully cultivate newly collected orchids.

## Adapting the Climate

In the early nineteenth century, equatorial zones were thought to be uniformly hot, damp, and shady. Struggling horticulturists and gardeners extended this concept in the creation of the stove house to emulate the sticky Tropics. Very little light and less air were admitted. The "stove" label came from the coal fire kept constantly burning to build a constant and oppressive heat.

Newly collected epiphytic orchids, often originating at higher elevations, were planted in peat beds where more often than not, they quickly expired. Sometimes they would give a last chance flower before dying. It was not to the advantage of the commercial collectors to be very specific about the habitats where they found any particular plant.

Once more information about habitats began to filter out, primarily from the botanists like John Lindley, growers learned that epiphytic orchids preferred having their roots exposed. Their native perches were emulated by placing the imported plants onto sticks or limbs with some mossy material to bind them in. This worked, after a fashion.

The revolution came when Lindley suggested to Paxton that the admission of outside air would create the buoyant and fresh atmosphere similar to orchids' native habitats. Paxton was the first to succeed with previously intractable plants, and his results were impressive.

The first notice of this method was published in the influential *Gardener's Chronicle* in 1859. One can certainly understand the excitement and satisfaction of finally seeing your plants, after decades of failure, prosper and thrive. And the plants would live not just for a few months, but as long as the grower cared for them.

Once this concept became more widely known, growers began to create environments that were cooler for the higher elevation plants and warmer for those from lower elevations. England, once known as the "Graveyard of Tropical Orchids," went on to lead the Western world in the cultivation and exhibition of fine, new varieties.

## Early Orchid Nurseries

From the earliest days of the eighteenth century until the period between the two World Wars, the orchid hobby was strictly the pursuit of the landed rich who were able to finance collecting expeditions to newly discovered lands where they hoped to obtain something choice with which to impress their wealthy peers. Estate gardeners, already responsible for cut flowers and vegetables, were then charged with learning how to care for orchid plants.

The earliest orchid sellers evolved from seed merchants into more general tropical nurseries where the discerning wealthy could obtain the latest palm as well as the newest and best from the orchid family. The same collectors searching the world for orchids also sought other desirable exotics and a logical partnership was established. One of the earliest successful purveyors of orchids and fine tropicals were Messrs. Conrad Loddiges in Hackney, founded in 1812 and active until the dissemination of their collection in 1852. It was they who displayed the plant that first caught the fancy of Lord Cavendish.

James Vietch and Sons, which began as a seed nursery in 1802, evolved into one of the most famous and influential of all orchid nurseries. Vietch's nursery was responsible for a breakthrough that would change orchid history. Dr. John Harris, a physician, had worked out how to successfully pollinate an orchid flower and suggested to Vietch's foreman the process that would ultimately lead to the creation of tens of thousands of hybrid orchids and the broad spectrum of flowers we know today. John Dominy, the foreman, made a series of hybrids that culminated with the first flowering, in 1856, of an artificial orchid hybrid, later to be named *Calanthe Dominyi*.

Other hybrids soon followed and the race was on. At the time of these groundbreaking achievements, the genetic affinities of various orchid species had yet to be appraised. Successful seed culture was hit and miss, although occasional success did occur by sowing the seed around the base of the mother plant. It is difficult to recapture the excitement and acclaim which followed the making of a hybrid, persuading the seed to grow into plants and tending them until they proved their unique qualities.

## Sander's List

There were other influential English firms during this developmental phase. The House of Sander came along in 1860, and rivaled, at its peak, the Vietch firm. Sander was vitally important in its provision of new species and hybrids, being ultimately responsible for some of today's best orchids through their development of early breeding lines. However, their work on *Sander's List of Orchid Hybrids* is where their name will live forever. The Sander family was the shepherd of this unique work until it was turned over to the Royal Horticultural Society in 1961. *Sander's List* is one of the aspects of orchidology that sets it apart in the world of horticulture. No other family of plants has the same complete and transparent record of hybrids made since, in essence, the dawn of time.

In the latter years of the nineteenth century, when records were incomplete and often conflicting, Sander had to first gather and sort existing records before order could be imposed. Today, thanks to the House of Sander, we can trace the full lineage of almost any orchid registered, from the first in 1856 with *Cal. Dominyi*, to today with the most complex hybrid *Phalaenopsis* or *Paphiopedilum* genera whose lineage may go back a dozen or more generations to the species.

## Germination Pioneers

Charlesworth & Co., founded in the waning years of the nineteenth century, was the first to employ truly modern seed culture techniques. Specializing in *Odontoglossum crispum* collected at higher elevations in Colombia, it made a business of obtaining the very finest varieties. Truly commercial production of large quantities of seedlings resulted from its collaboration with a Dr. Ramsbottom, who helped to perfect the symbiotic method of orchid culture.

As discussed elsewhere, orchid seed germinates in close association with a symbiotic fungus that provides nutrition to the developing seedling. In the late nineteenth century seed was sown around a mother plant and germinated with some limited success, owing to the presence of the necessary mycorhizal fungus originating in the wild-collected plant.

Recently gained knowledge of the presence and function of the invading fungus was the basis of Charlesworth's and Ramsbottom's success. After isolation of the appropriate and necessary strain of fungus, the sterilized seedling media was inoculated with the fungus. It was quickly discovered that this method, properly executed, germinated orchid seed freely and in quantities much greater than ever expected. From the occasional one or a dozen orchid seedlings closely held and seldom released, Charlesworth had found the first of many mother lodes of orchid hybridization, not only leading to the sensational "odonts" we know today, but pointing toward modern industrial orchid production.

## The English Legacy

The collection of Sir George Holford at Westonbirt, tended by his grower, H. G. Alexander, can be seen as representing the final step in reaching our modern orchid world. Many claim that Alexander is the greatest hybridizer of all time. His manifold hybrids include *Cymbidium* Alexanderi 'Westonbirt,' *Lc.* Lustre 'Westonbirt,' and *Paph.* Hellas 'Westonbirt' and their countless progeny. It was Alexander who trained the grower who would transform America's concept of commercial orchid growing. B. O. Bracey, through his association with Armacost & Royston, would usher in the modern era of mass orchid production.

In Bracey, we have the culmination and final stage of the evolution of the orchid grower from estate gardener, to nurseryman growing wild-collected plants, to the truly commercial nurseryman specializing in the hybridization and cultivation of hybrid orchid plants. The many nurserymen trained by Bracey formed the core of the American orchid industry in the immediate post-War era. This same era was to see the eclipse of the English as influential in the world orchid scene. The effect of two World Wars was to force many nurseries into a position where they could not economically operate. The United States, repository of their best and brightest talent, took the lead. This leadership was based on good English hybrids, and the much more favorable climate and a larger market which drove American commercial exploitation of orchid hybrids.

## American Orchid Culture

American orchid culture had gotten its start in the middle years of the nineteenth century, when the wealthy followed every English fad, including their hobbies. Commercial orchid growing was somewhat slower to develop in the U.S.

One of the earliest American orchid nurseries was Butterworth's in Massachusetts. As in England, much of early American orchid growing was focused on the supply to the "aristocracy." Hence, most of the pioneering orchid

**Right:** The White House orchid conservatory was one of the specialist plant conservatories added to the president's residence in the 1870s and 1880s, alongside structures for camellias, roses, and bedding plants. All were swept aside to make way for the West Wing in 1902.

nurseries were in the Northeast. Although some early attempts were made in the Deep South and Florida, it was not until air conditioning made living more practical that any real industry could be realized.

Modern orchid growing began in 1922. Dr. Louis Knudson of Cornell University, building on the same research used by Charlesworth and Ramsbottom in their symbiotic approach to orchid seedling culture, devised the asymbiotic method, and modern orchid growing began. Subsequently, Knudson went west to California, to Armacost & Royston of Sawtelle, and taught B. O. Bracey his methods. Armacost, whose orchid business built on the famous Doheny collection which it had purchased some years previously and the association of Bracey with Alexander, created a maelstrom of hybrid orchid seedling production.

This hybrid seedling production boom would lead to the enormous orchid cut flower industry of the World War II years. Bracey's unparalleled observational powers, coupled with his access to the best of English breeding and the ability to grow thousands of any hybrid, led to the selection of highly superior and advanced breeding plants, which rapidly accelerated the development of orchids. Armacost became the powerhouse of a new orchid industry in the U.S.

### From Cut Flowers to Plants
Armacost's production of orchid seedlings fueled a rapidly growing and very profitable market in cut-orchid blooms, especially cattleyas. Because the flowers were so profitable, orchid plants were not widely available to the public in the years between the wars. Demand for orchid cut flowers built over the years and nurseries such as George E. Baldwin, Thomas Young, and The Rod McLellan Co. capitalized on this highly profitable and exclusive market.

Demand peaked during World War II when, for the first time in many years, the working class had excess income available for frivolities such as orchid plants. Demand for orchid cut flowers, primarily cattleyas, but later cymbidiums, waned over the years, until, by the latter part of the twentieth century, the orchid cut-flower industry was but a shadow of its former self. During this period, orchid production shifted to more hobby-oriented types and the gradual evolution of orchids suitable as flowering potted plants. Excess cut flower stock was spun off as potted plants more widely available to the masses. A big

step in this process was the formation of the American Orchid Society in 1921.

Formed by wealthy Easterners and the orchid nurseries that supplied them, its original intent was to fight the onset of a proposed quarantine of imported orchids, then the mainstay of the orchid industry. The AOS morphed after World War II into an organization intimately concerned with the popularization of the orchid hobby. Thanks to its prescient editor and executive director, Gordon Dillon, the AOS has played and continues to play a significant role.

### A New Medium
The last cultural breakthrough that enabled far more to enjoy successful orchid culture came about in the early 1950s. John Ivory, a lumber mill owner, began to look for other uses for his mill's waste products. He enlisted the help of O. A. Matkin of California's Soil and Plant Laboratory. Both became convinced that the bark stripped from the logs in the milling process could be used in orchid culture. This came at a critical point in the nursery business. Osmunda, the fern roots that had long been used for growing orchid plants, was becoming increasingly scarce and was of decreasing quality, and rapidly escalating cost. Nor was it the easiest material for amateurs to pot with and grow in.

Matkin and O. W. Davidson of Rutgers University conducted initial, highly favorable, tests that showed the potential of the new medium. With increased processing and suitable fertilizers, fir bark became the potting medium of choice for the next 40 years, with its ease of use enabling the rapid growth of the hobby-orchid industry.

### Rise and Fall of the Orchid Nurseries
This hobby industry has been served by an increasingly sophisticated coterie of specialist nurseries. Some of these nurseries were founded on the collections of the wealthy—Fred A. Stewart, Inc., Jones & Scully, Kensington Orchids—some grew out of previously successful cut-flower nurseries—Armacost & Royston, Rod McLellan Co., Carter & Holmes—while others were begun simply as a way to support and justify an out-of-control hobby.

Many nurseries thrived during the decades of the 60s through the 90s. This was an era of specialization and personal service by the independent nursery operators. The businesses were often vertically integrated, with unique breeding lines developed over a period of decades and used

to develop new products. These new products were offered in splashy and sophisticated mail-order catalogs.

During this period, cloning became an important process. First developed by Morel in France as a method to create and propagate virus-free potatoes, meristemming, as it has become known in orchid circles, was an extraordinarily useful tool in the replication of exact varieties for resale.

Hybrid orchids do not come true from seed, showing a bell curve type variation from extremely poor to a vast middle ground of average examples and a few superb plants. Perhaps only one or two out of a thousand might ever be considered as award winners. Until the early 1970s, these few plants could only be propagated by division, resulting in very expensive plants. With the advent of meristemming, growers could, over the period of a few years, manufacture hundreds of precise replicas.

**Above:** *Paphiopedilum lowii* has been regularly used by nurserymen for orchid hybridization from the 1870s to the present day.

Distribution was still at premium prices, of course, but far below former levels.

Sadly, over the past 15 years or so, we have seen many of the formerly great orchid nurseries fall by the wayside. A changing market and the associated economic pressures have driven many out of the business. Offshore growers, with the advantage of lower costs and looking to continue their rapid growth, are invading the U.S. These offshore growers came first looking to U.S. nurseries to finish, bring into flower, their plants and are now establishing facilities here in the U.S. to compete with American growers. As a result, domestic orchid nurseries are beset on all sides by competition from homegrown garden centers and the large home centers.

# WHAT IS AN ORCHID?

*Despite their reputation as exotic subtropical plants, orchids are found in a huge range of climatic conditions and range in size from less than an inch to over twenty feet high.*

Orchids share a variety of distinctive floral and vegetative features. The gestalt of an orchid plant's appearance is often sufficiently characteristic that even moderately experienced orchidists have little trouble saying some new plant or other "looks like an orchid."

Most popularly cultivated orchids are epiphytes, meaning "upon a tree," and in natural settings grow in the forest canopy, using the dominant trees as support. This is a rather common adaptation to overcome insufficient light and nutrients on the woodland floor. Up in the canopy, light, while dappled, is stronger and more available and water and nutrients are captured by craggy bark and detritus accumulations in the forks of tree branches. A typical tropical or subtropical forest environment would include as epiphytes such familiar plants as begonias, bromeliads, gesneriads (African violets and their relatives), ferns, cacti, peperomias, and tradescantias (Wandering Jews) growing alongside orchids.

Of course not all orchids look alike. They exhibit a range of size and foliar features that are second to none. However, there is a shared set of characters that enables easy discernment of an orchid plant whether *in situ* or at the garden center. The most recognizable characteristic, and the most commonly seen in orchids, is the fleshy velamen-covered roots.

## Orchid Roots

Velamen is a spongy, water-absorbent tissue that surrounds the root core. This tissue catches the first, nutrient-rich moisture available, whether from rainfall, nightly dew, or irrigation. It also traps trace amounts of moisture in the sometimes-marginal habitats where orchids are often found. Velamen is also present in most terrestrial orchids.

This is because orchids that grow *on* the ground in nature often do not really grow *in* the ground. Their roots ramble about in the nutritious forest duff where air circulation is plentiful and moisture available, even if only in small amounts. There are also many truly terrestrial orchids, whose roots do actually penetrate into the soil substrate. However, these usually grow in a complex symbiotic relationship with the native soil flora and fauna and are generally quite difficult to grow in cultivation.

From this one character, we can project a cultivated orchid plant's need for an open potting medium that allows the retention of a moderate amount of moisture as well as air circulation. If the potting medium is kept constantly wet, the roots drown from lack of gas exchange. For both epiphytic and terrestrial orchids, the velamen-coated roots are key to an amazing capacity to thrive in habitats that would otherwise be considered marginal.

The roots of epiphytic orchids take many forms and serve a broad variety of functions. Whether rounded and rambling, seemingly unattached to the substrate, or flattened and ranging about the bark of the host tree, the roots function to both hold the plant tight to the surface and to seek out whatever ephemeral moisture and nutrients may be available. The roots of epiphytic orchids are often fat and succulent, serving as additional water and nutrient storage. They may even have chlorophyll and be photosynthetic, allowing the plant to do without leaves entirely. For example, *Polyradicion gracilis* does very well with no leaves at all, albeit in humid areas.

---

**Right:** Members of the leafless genus *Polyradicion* (now *Dendrophylax*) such as *Polyradicion lindenii*, photosynthesize through chlorophyl in the roots.

Finally, there are orchids—*Ansellia, Cyrtopodium, Grammatophyllum,* among others—that have what are known as bird's nest roots, which project upward in a distinctive mass and serve to catch debris, that both nourishes the plant and serves as a water catchment system. In some species, such as *Phalaenopsis schilleriana* and *Phal. stuartiana,* orchid roots have evolved adventitious buds that form into plantlets, thereby asexually propagating the plant over a favorable area.

Well-developed foliar water-storage orchids, such as those with thickened stems (pseudobulbs), fleshy leaves, and thick, water-resistant cuticles, team up with orchid roots to make orchids among the most hardy and adaptable of all flowering plants.

**Terrestrial Orchids**

While a significant proportion of popularly cultivated orchids are epiphytic, even though they are grown in pots for convenience, there are a good number of true terrestrial plants. For example, some of the best known and most widely grown (where conditions permit) of all orchids, Cymbidium, come from the rich duff that accumulates on the forest floor.

Thick, fleshy roots perform an array of functions for the plant, from anchorage to storage of water and nutrients. Sobralias, noted by their reed-like stems and pleated, alternating leaves, are common at mid-elevations through the New World tropics. These make some of the most beautiful orchid plants of all, they resemble compact clumps of bamboo, hence, their popular name of bamboo orchids. The large, generally short-lived cattleya-like blooms are borne in succession from the apex of the canes. Their roots are among the most robust of all terrestrial orchids, highly succulent and profuse. Sadly, transplanting this type of plant from the wild into cultivation is especially difficult owing to the vital role played by the roots, which are easily damaged and lost in transit or transplanting.

As with sobralias, many terrestrials do not have well-developed foliar water storage schemes and so rely almost entirely on their fleshy roots for sustenance during hard climatic times. The best-known examples of this type are the several genera of slipper orchids (*Paphiopedilum, Phragmipedium,* and *Cypripedium*). Many temperate zone terrestrials also fall into this category. While most commonly grown slippers are not seasonally deciduous, many other terrestrial orchids are, doubling up on adaptive schemes by counting on their fleshy root masses to carry them over the dry, cold, or otherwise unfavorable seasons.

The deciduous terrestrials also live in a very close relationship with the soil fauna of their environment and so are very difficult to cultivate even by the most dedicated. The slippers, however, tend to be plants whose roots ramble through the forest duff and are more easily cultivated than many other true terrestrials.

## Growth Habits

Orchids exhibit two primary growth habits—sympodial (primitive) and monopodial (derived). The sympodial habit involves the plant producing a more or less elongated—in some cases, nearly invisible—horizontal rhizome from the base of which new growths emerge. Most gardeners are familiar with ginger, irises, or bamboo, which also show this growth habit. Flowering stems may appear from the apex of the newest growth or from the axils of the leaves. The growths may be succulent, with pronounced thickening to form pseudobulbs for storage—*Cattleya* is an excellent example of this—or may have soft leaves arranged more or less in a fan as in *Paphiopedilum*.

Monopodial orchids, in contrast, grow straight up along a stem, with one main terminal apex. Branching may occur anywhere along the stem from either the leaf axil or opposite it, but there is generally a dominant stem. Flowering stems emerge from the axils of the leaves which develop continuously from the active growth point. As with a palm tree, growth is straight up. Vandas and phalaenopsis are commonly seen monopodial orchids.

## Flower Form

Few orchids, however, are grown simply for the leaves. Perhaps the notable exceptions to this rule are the many jewel orchids, such as *Anoectochilus* and *Ludisia* with richly veined nearly black leaves. It is the blooms that set orchids apart from other, more prosaic, flowering potted plants. The profusion of richly colored and exotically marked flowers have placed many under their spell.

What sets these regal blossoms apart from other blooms? Orchids, being monocots (monocots is short for monocotyledonous plants that have one cotyledon, or embryonic leaf, in their seed), have flowers arranged in whorls of three. Three sepals on the outer whorl encase the inner whorl of three petals.

One of the showiest aspects of almost any orchid flower is the lip, or labellum, a highly modified third petal, often the lowest, which serves as a pollinator-attracting device. Orchid lips have evolved a diverse array of wild and wonderful ways to attract and trap various animals—birds, bees, moths, bats, gnats, and others—into pollinating their flowers. The lip is generally considered to be the lowermost of the three petals, because orchids are usually resupinate, or appearing to be upside down. The flower stem twists

Above: *Cypripedium acaule* is a terrestrial slipper orchid found throughout much of the eastern United States. It relies on thick roots to obtain moisture and nutrients from the forest duff.

180 degrees during development to present the lip, which develops at the top of the bloom, at the bottom. Orchids that present the lip uppermost twist through 360 degrees!

The lip encloses the most complex of the orchid's adaptive features, the column, which unites the male stamens and the female stigmatic surface into one. There is a strong evolutionary advantage to this arrangement.

Orchids have fine, dust-like seeds that are produced in vast numbers—a single seedpod may contain literally millions of seed to be spread by wind. The object is for one or a few to find just the right spot to germinate and grow.

Because so many seed need to be fertilized, a mechanism that guarantees the precise placement of enough individual pollen grains to fertilize each ovule is essential. Orchid pollen grains are bound together in two or four large masses called pollinia.

The column of the orchid bloom is adapted to allow placement of a high number of pollen grains precisely where the pollen tubes can successfully fertilize the concentrated ovules. The pollinaria are constructed to avoid self-fertilization, which is evolutionarily undesirable. This is generally accomplished by movement of the stem—twisting, bending, and turning—after removal from the column, from a position where self-fertilization is improbable, to one where cross-pollination is possible.

Another structure that helps to prevent self-pollination is the rostellum, a barrier between the pollinia and stigmatic surface. In self-pollinating orchids, premature drying of the rostellum allows self-pollination before the flower opens. Self-fertilization does occasionally occur in orchids, sometimes intentionally, but is normally as undesirable in orchids as it is in any other organism.

## Extreme Orchids

Orchids have evolved into one of the largest of all plant families with over 25,000 naturally occurring species discovered to date by a process of relatively rapid speciation, events that cause a species to split into two separate genetic lines, and habitat radiation, their spread through a habitat, is responsible for their numbers.

Orchids inhabit an incredibly wide range of habitats, many of them very localized. There are surely many orchids still to be discovered, and many, owing to habitat loss, that will never be known. As orchids have evolved, the variety of plant forms and habits has grown to fill just about every imaginable niche and to give every competitive advantage.

The largest orchids are truly massive, such as the tropical *Grammatophyllum speciosum* and *Gram. papuanum*, which can reach several yards in height and weigh over a ton when mature. Height is not the only extreme for giant orchids. Sometimes sheer mass is the

criteria, as in the various vining members of the genus *Vanilla*, whose overall weight would be difficult to calculate because the vines can reach many feet in length. One nursery-grown plant was over 400 feet long before it flowered for the first time. Recently discovered New World sobralias can be over 20 feet (6 meters) tall! Of course, many orchids are simply large plants, such as *Cattleya guttata*, which can reach over six feet (180 cms) in height. However, even more are minuscule, such as some of the smallest known of all orchid plants, *Platystele jungermannoides* and *Bulbophyllum odoardii*, both at less than one quarter of an inch (0.5 cms). Some orchids are true giants and some are true dwarfs, with the vast majority fitting somewhere in between six inches to three feet (10 cms to one meter).

One of the best known at the smaller end of the scale, popular with indoor growers short on space, is *Pleurothallis grobyi*. This plant is representative of an entire group of miniature orchids, which inspire almost fanatic devotion among windowsill growers because so many plants can be crammed into such a compact space.

Certainly the strangest of the many habitats that orchids occupy is underground. The subterranean *Rhizanthella*, of Australia, is never seen above ground, with its flowers only appearing when temporarily uncovered at the surface by rooting animals. Another type of subterranean orchid is the saprophytic type, which lives off rotting vegetation in the soil substrate, not unlike fungi, with only the flower spikes emerging to show that there are orchid plants in occupation.

## Orchid Range

Orchids are often identified with tropical or subtropical areas. However, with a cosmopolitan range from northern Sweden and Alaska to Tierra del Fuego and Macquarie Island; from sea level to over 12,000 feet (3,657 meters) in the Andes, orchids are one of the widest ranging of all plant families. Indeed, according to Robert Dressler, orchids occupy habitats that are "near the limits of vegetation."

The habitat preference of any given orchid has a profound influence on its cultivation. Surprisingly, many orchids have evolved great stress tolerance, and an almost "weedy" habit. This type is often among the first to colonize disturbed or marginal habitats such as road cuts, slopes damaged by landslides, or new volcanic islands. For

example, zygopetalums are commonly seen in roadside ditches in Brazil, with their leaves sawn off by road maintenance, flower stems emerging proudly from developing growths. On a road cut in Colombia, experts were puzzled by what were clearly orchid seedlings popping up in the clay soil of a recent road cut, only to discern that they were *Phragmipedium* seedlings from seed rained down from a mother plant above the cut.

Such early habitat colonists are the "coyotes" of the orchid world because of their amazing ability to exploit changing conditions, whether the result of human intervention or natural catastrophe. Not unlike coyotes, which have easily adapted and spread with man's changing environment, many orchids are denizens of the changing environment, taking advantage of the temporary clearing of an area before a shadier climax community can emerge and crowd them out.

**Above:** Shown here is a typical spotted *Rhynchostylia gigantea* flower. It can also be found in dark red, pink, and white forms.

It must be stressed, however, there are also "panda" orchids: orchids that have evolved such a high degree of interdependence with their environment that any change—rainfall, shade or sun, pollinator—leads to their rapid decline and possible extinction. Generally, these plants are the exception, but they can and do serve as the poster children for habitat preservation, much as pandas do in the animal kingdom.

## Photosynthetic Process

In addition to their many anatomic adaptations that allow survival in marginal environments, many orchids have a very stress-tolerant metabolism known as CAM. This is a photosynthetic pathway that produces one metabolic product during daylight hours when moisture stress may be limiting, and completes the pathway during darkness hours, when the leaf cells can be open for gas and moisture exchange without overly taxing the plant's moisture reserves. This metabolic mechanism is especially favorable for epiphytic orchids, where moisture is often limiting during the warmer daylight hours and where humidity rises as temperature drops at night, allowing condensation to recharge the moisture-absorbing velamen of the roots.

## Finding Their Niche

As previously noted, orchid seed is very fine and dustlike. Essentially it contains no endosperm, the starchy, nutritive material that gives most angiosperm seedlings the energy to germinate and grow until their own photosynthetic pathways begin to function. In nature, orchid seed must be invaded by the mycorhizae, fungi, whose metabolic by-products are nutritive to the young plant and enable the orchid seedling to germinate and begin growth. Such explicit conditions only exist in a limited number of

Below: At the opposite end of the scale *Pleurothallis grobyi* is one of the smallest orchids, allowing windowsill growers to maximise their growing pace with a large number of different plants.

places—just the right tree, the most favorable soil, a crack in a rock—and so only a very small percentage of seed ever germinates from any seedpod.

In nature this can lead to a particular tree being an "orchid tree," or to a species being locally abundant, where the conditions are just right. This aspect of orchid ecology profoundly influences not only orchids' distribution within a given habitat, but their cultivation.

The complex syndrome of adaptations necessary for the epiphytic habit has many consequences both for the student of the plants and the grower. Why, exactly, did orchids begin to grow high in the forest canopy, using the trees for support? If you think about a tropical or subtropical forest as a whole, you may begin to see the reasons more easily. Nearly all of the biomass—the available nutrients—of such a forest is tied up in the existing vegetation. When a tree falls, forest microorganisms quickly recycle it, leaving very little to go back into the soil. The many layers of forest canopy filter photosynthetic rays extremely efficiently, allowing very few to reach the lowest floor level.

Most have an image of a natural forest being a solid, impenetrable tangle of branches from top to bottom. Actually, the floor of a forest can be open and nearly sterile, park-like in its appearance. Even when enough light penetrates to the forest floor to support the growth of some herbaceous plants, the competition for scarce nutrients is fierce. How, then, can a plant compete? By moving up into the canopy itself, where it can capture both light and nutrients before they are filtered out by larger plants.

Tropical and subtropical orchids in many cases live in the trees, stratified according to their light needs from the highest perches at the fringes of the forest—where light is intense and moisture less dependable—to further down in the canopy where light is of lower intensity but moisture and nutrients are more constant.

The plant habit of any given orchid will often reflect its preferred position in the forest. Succulent leaves with a waxy protective cuticle team with swollen water-retentive pseudobulbs to support plants exposed to brighter light and drier conditions. Softer, broader leaves and less conspicuous water-storage organs are the norm on plants in shadier, moister environments. These and other clues give the experienced orchid grower a wealth of information on the successful culture of an unknown plant and where to place it in the home or greenhouse.

# BASIC GROWING REQUIREMENTS

*To become a successful orchid grower, it's important to learn the roles played by light, air, water, and nutrients in maintaining healthy and blooming orchid plants.*

The basic requirements for the growth of orchids—or of any plant—cannot be separated one from the other but must be taken as a whole. A surfeit of one is nearly always as bad, or worse, than a shortage of another. Nor are there any hard and fast rules that can serve the novice as magic bullets to successful orchid culture. There is no one combination of factors, precisely delineated, that is the right way to grow orchids. However, a foundation of understanding about each of the individual factors and how each contributes to the well-being of the plant will enable the aspiring grower to produce good-quality plants with the best quality flowers.

First and foremost, the grower has to be concerned with the health and well-being of the plant. An unhealthy plant will not produce blooms. Even if it does flower, the blooms will be of indifferent quality and quickly wither and fade. Blooms also undermine the already precarious state of the plant.

This is an important lesson. An orchid flower needs to attract pollinators, set viable seed, and perpetuate the species—not because it is happy, not from sheer *joie de vivre*, not to look pretty or smell good. An orchid flowers to attract pollinators, period. This takes energy. Energy that a weak plant can ill afford.

Sometimes the biological imperative to set seed overcomes the individual plant's need to survive, and the plant flowers, even if the flowering means that the plant will die. So, if a weak plant throws up a flower stem, it is not because it is—despite appearances to the contrary—doing better, but because it is about to die.

Other orchids, notably moth orchids (*Phalaenopsis*), will continue to flower over a long period of time, branching from old stems, until all the plant's energy is used up and the plant dies. The bottom line is that if a

plant looks poorly, it shouldn't be allowed to flower. Remove the emerging inflorescence as an investment in the plant's future. On the other hand, plants that look too healthy or too green and soft will not flower either. This will be discussed below under "Light."

## Light

Lack of good quality light is the most common limiting factor in home orchid growing. When a plant does not flower in its season, the reason is, more often than not, that it is not getting enough light of sufficient quality.

A common mistake made by beginners is to believe that quantity of light—providing longer hours—will make up for poor quality light. Nothing could be further from the truth. Indeed, overlong hours of light, even of the dimmest sort, interrupt an orchid plant's metabolic patterns so that both flowering and growing are disrupted. Much like too little sleep robs your body of the opportunity to rest and metabolize, resulting in "burn out," so will similar circumstances hurt your orchids' performance. Anything over 15 or so hours of light is both unnecessary and harmful. Even the equivalent of a 60-watt lightbulb, left on during nighttime hours, is enough to cause an interruption in normal metabolism.

Symptoms of overlong daylight hours appear similar to other stress-related culture problems. These include leaf tip burn or blackening, weak growths, and lack of flowers. The plants often will appear to be desiccated and flaccid. Seasonal variation in day length, as in nature, is often a necessary factor in triggering plants into seasonal flowering. Most growers, however, unless they grow strictly under lights in a basement or other protected area, do not need to concern themselves with this problem. As long as the plants get about the same hours of light in your growing area as they might out of doors at that same time, they will be fine. If supplemental hours of light are provided during dimmer winter hours, try to restrict them to a total of not more that 14 to 15 hours in aggregate with daylight hours.

But what is good quality light? How can a grower know if he has light of adequate quality? Remember that orchids —especially the most commonly cultivated types—have evolved to grow in locations that enable them to take advantage of the best available light. Whether they are terrestrial types adapted to growing rapidly in spots in the forest where there is a sudden break in the canopy or epiphytic, living high in the canopy where light is less filtered by other plants, orchids grow best in strong, dappled light. As you walk through a forest there are changing light patterns, caused by the differing layers of foliage about you. Light is stronger in some places, weaker in others. This dappled sunlight, never too strong in any one place on the plant, is ideal for growing strong, healthy orchid plants.

While some growers prefer to rely on the purely objective measurements provided by light meters to gauge light intensity, more experienced growers learn to judge light quality by the appearance of their plants and by other methods that do not require technology.

The best growers have compared their observations against light meters often enough to have a good idea of what the light conditions are in any given situation. Remember, too, that owing to the variety of other factors that affect how a plant reacts, numbers on a gauge don't tell the whole story. Learn to know the light level in an area by close observation backed up, if you wish, by a commercially available light meter.

The angle of the sun changes throughout the year. As the days grow longer from spring into summer and the sun rises higher in the sky, longer daylight hours couple with more intense irradiation of the sun's rays to cause sunburn, unless carefully monitored. Conversely, as days shorten as fall merges into winter, the sun's angle gets lower, with shorter days and less intense, i.e. lower quality, light.

An African violet, costing about $2, can serve as a "canary in a coal mine" to see if your light is of sufficient quality and quantity for orchid culture. If the violet remains in flower in your designated area during most of the year— even a violet will stop flowering during the very shortest days of winter—you can grow orchids. However, for those

**Above:** *Cattleya mossiae* is a typical epiphyte, seen here colonizing a tree in Venezuela. It was the second unifoliate cattleya species to be described and is the national flower of Venezuela.

who want the technical reassurance, light meters work and can be bought for around $30. As a very broad rule, the light level required for the following families are:

*Phalaenopsis* 10,000 to 15,000 Lux

*Dendrobium* 15,000 to 25,000 Lux

*Cattleya* 20,000 to 30,000 Lux

*Paphiopedilum* 10,000 to 15,000 Lux

*Oncidium* 20,000 to 50,000 Lux

Plants that receive light appropriate to their type are strong and healthy with medium green foliage and pseudobulbs that support themselves upright without need of staking or other support. Each growth, or leaf in the case of monopodial types, will be appropriately larger than the preceding until the mature size is reached. Flower stems are thick and may also be to a great extent self-supporting. Flower production, whether few or many, will be close to the full potential of the particular plant. If a plant is leggy, floppy, or otherwise unable to support its own foliar mass, chances are that it is not receiving enough light. There are certain orchids for which you will simply never be able to provide proper light, owing to the particular conditions of your environment or climate.

Similarly, it is important to assess whether your plants are receiving too *much* light. If the plants seem bleached or, under more extreme conditions, scorched, the chances are that the light has gotten too bright. Even when heat is not a factor—as it will be under some high-light conditions—excess light will cause the chlorophyll to bleach out and stress the plants, preventing them from reaching their potential.

You are more likely to see this sort of damage as the seasons change from winter to spring, especially when the bright sun breaks through the cloud cover after rain, when the atmosphere is unusually clear, and/or the plants have not acclimatized to the higher light intensities after winter.

Whenever moving your plants from lower to higher light regimes—either naturally as the seasons progress, or simply by moving closer to the window—do it gradually, as you would on your first days at the beach after a long winter. Just like you, the plants will be softer and more susceptible to burning. However, the general rule of thumb should be to provide your plants with as much light as they can stand.

Ideal light conditions are not always possible, because the plants are grown indoors or in areas where the light cannot be easily controlled. Under the best circumstances, you will need to moderate your light intensity by shade of some sort because it is always easier to provide more shade than more light. In the home, an east window is considered ideal, while a lightly shaded (by a sheer curtain, for example) south window is a close second. A west exposure will work, but heat buildup is more likely from the late afternoon sun than with the other exposures. A northern exposure will almost never work for anything but "foliage" orchids, such as jewel orchids.

If one is lucky enough to have a sunroom with overhead light or a full compliment of windows around the perimeter, the variety of orchids that may be grown is large. A greenhouse provides the widest array of artificially controllable environments. Many growers are lucky enough to live in areas where orchids can be grown out of doors on their patios at least part of the year. Some live in frost-free

**Above:** This orchid is showing signs of extreme stress having been bleached by excessive light.

It is appropriate to discuss temperature under the topic of light. Light, from the sun or other sources, provides the bulk of heat available during daylight hours. When the sun is at a higher angle during the summer months, light is more intense because it encounters less atmospheric interference. As the sun sinks lower toward the horizon with the approach of fall, the light is of lower energy from the increased atmospheric interference it encounters. This also explains why the incident (angled) light that comes into your home is of lower quality than that which comes from overhead in a sunroom or greenhouse. As light strikes a surface, it is reflected and re-radiated in lower infrared wavelengths or, in lay terms, heat.

This is how a greenhouse works. The visible light of the sun easily penetrates the glass or other transparent covering of the greenhouse, but the covering retains the re-radiated infrared waves, or heat. Enough has been written on the greenhouse effect caused by increasing carbon dioxide emissions for most people to be familiar with the phenomenon.

Because the sun provides the bulk of the daytime heat, it is natural for heat to increase during daylight hours and begin to fall as the sun sets. This completely natural diurnal variation in temperatures is critical to the health of your orchids. A minimum of a 15° Fahrenheit (8° Celsius) variation is essential to allowing orchids' metabolism to function properly. Whether in the home or in the greenhouse, if night temperatures are kept artificially high in relation to day temperatures, orchid health will suffer.

If sunlight-aided day temperatures are not rising out of the 60s Fahrenheit (15–20° Celsius), it is safe to allow the nights to sink into the middle 50s Fahrenheit (13° Celsius), providing watering and fertilizing are held in check as well.

Conversely, when days rise naturally into the 80s and 90s Fahrenheit (26–35° Celsius) with higher night temperatures, plant growth will be rapid, but water and fertilizer application frequency will need to increase to keep pace. In lower temperature situations, if a grower provides the same level of fertilizer and water as during warmer, brighter months, the least of the problems will be forced, soft growth, and the worst will be damage associated with bacterial and other diseases of soft growth.

The particular temperature regime preferred by any given orchid is highly dependent on its native environment. Most of the commonly cultivated orchids come from the middle elevations of the tropics and subtropics where night

areas, such as south Florida or the West Coast, where there is a great tradition of growing plants out of doors year round. Actually, those who can grow their plants out of doors at least part, if not all, of the year have an advantage over the greenhouse grower because they can take advantage of naturally occurring light levels and gentle, cooling breezes that must be duplicated in a greenhouse situation.

Those who must grow indoors through colder periods can often find an area outdoors for their orchids during frost-free months where enough good-quality growth allows them to succeed with a wide array of plants.

temperatures are commonly in the 60s Fahrenheit (15–20°Celsius), and days are comfortably in the 80s (26–35°Celsius). Such environments are found at sea level to perhaps 1000 feet (304 meters) in areas further from the equator, and at increasing elevations nearer to the equator.

Traditionally, there have been three general temperature regimes for orchids: cool, intermediate, and warm (or stove). Cool growing orchids are almost always from high elevations, where nights may dip into the 40s Fahrenheit (5–10°Celsius) and days rarely exceed 70°Fahrenheit (21°Celsius). These uniformly cool temperatures are accompanied by fairly high humidity (above 70 percent) and are usually fairly difficult to duplicate in the home, or in warmer climates.

As noted above, by far the majority of commonly seen orchids can be grown under intermediate, or cattleya-type, conditions. Here, nights are in the high 50s and low 60s Fahrenheit (15–20°Celsius), with days ranging into the 80s or even 90s (26–32°Celsius). Humidity, owing to the somewhat warmer temperatures and more air movement, is in the 60 percent range.

This type of environment is found at moderate elevations of 1,000–3,000 feet (300–900 meters), depending on how far from the equator the locale is found. This is the easiest and least costly temperature range to duplicate in the home or in the bulk of the U.S.

Finally, there are those orchids that come from low elevations in tropical areas close to the equator. Night temperatures may exceed 80°Fahrenheit (26° Celsius), while days may soar above 90°Fahrenheit (32°Celsius). Humidity is usually high, 70 or 80 percent or more. Light factors are very intense. This is where orchids like vandas and other monopodial types usually fall. Unless one lives in the subtropical areas of Florida and the Gulf States, these conditions can be very difficult and/or costly to duplicate in a greenhouse.

## Air

Any discussion about air consists of the dual topics of air movement and the constituent components of the atmosphere, particularly the role air movement plays in temperature and humidity control. Orchids, in general, require gently moving air around them, not only to help moderate temperature, but also to provide the carbon dioxide necessary for photosynthesis.

If air movement is inadequate, not only will carbon dioxide supplies become insufficient for plant respiration, but fungal and bacterial problems may arise as well. Even when grown in the home, orchids need some air movement around them. Except on the very coldest days, a window can be kept cracked somewhere in the room to provide some fresh air. When this is not possible, as may be the case in cold areas, a small oscillating fan can provide the needed air circulation.

In the greenhouse, fans are almost always necessary, both to move air around in the space and to prevent vertical stratification. In warm areas, this means keeping hot air from building up in the higher reaches of the growing area and allowing it to vent out the ridge while being replaced by cooler air from lower in the greenhouse.

Gentle air movement helps even out temperatures and humidity. Otherwise, the air high in the growing area may become superheated and dry while the lower areas are stagnant and subject to diseases that thrive in such close conditions. In situations where orchids are grown outdoors, too much air movement can become a problem, as in wind-prone areas. When air movement is extreme, the plant's abilities to maintain its moisture levels are taxed, and the resultant stress can lead to growth retardation.

It is good to remember that plants transpire through stomata, pore-like openings in the leaf surfaces. This transpiration not only provides gas exchange but also creates a microclimate of humidity immediately surrounding the leaf. When air movement is too brisk over too long a period of time, the plant simply cannot take up water quickly enough to compensate for the loss of moisture through the stomata. For this reason, if your plants are grown where the wind is likely to become a problem, it is advisable to provide some sort of windbreak.

## Water

Orchids need water at their roots and in the atmosphere. However, the degree to which any particular type needs moisture at the roots or in the air varies according to the environment from which it originates. Some types—cattleyas, equitant oncidiums, and others—originate from higher in the forest canopy, where brisk air movement and high light result in rapid drying of the roots, even if atmospheric moisture remains good. Others—brassias, phalaenopsis, huntleyas, and similar types—grow further

**Right:** To determine if your orchid needs watering, use the skewer test. Push a pencil, or wooden skewer, into the medium to about 2" (5cms). If it looks moist when it is removed, then don't water. If it doesn't, check by rolling it on your arm or cheek. If it feels cool and moist, still don't water. If it feels warm and dry, get the watering can out.

down in the canopy where shadier and more sheltered conditions allow moisture to remain around the roots longer while humidity also remains high. While some orchids will do better with higher humidity—particularly those without well-developed water storage organs, such as phalaenopsis and vandas—most will do quite well with an average relative humidity of 50 to 60 percent.

What is relative humidity, or RH? A set volume of air, at a set temperature, holds a set volume of water. The warmer the air, the more water it can potentially hold; the cooler the air, the less it can hold. Thus, for a set volume of air with a fixed amount of water held in it, as temperature rises, the relative humidity falls. As the temperature falls, the relative humidity rises.

Unfortunately, this relationship is opposite to that which orchids, and plants in general, prefer. Orchids do best if relative humidity rises and falls with temperature. Orchids would like to have higher humidity with higher temperatures. Some growers have misting systems installed in their greenhouses or growing areas (clearly not in home situations) that are humidistat-actuated to raise humidity during daylight hours when the grower may not be available. Unfortunately, while you can add water to raise relative humidity as temperatures rise, you cannot remove it to lower RH as temperatures fall. Air circulation and proper venting of the growing area will help to mitigate this problem to some extent, so management of air movement is critical to good growing. Thankfully, artificial heat also tends to lower humidity.

Of course, orchids also need water at their roots. The moisture available to the plants' roots provides the water necessary for the physiological processes of the plants. The moisture transpired by the stomata is what pulls water up through the vascular system of the plant. If the amount of moisture transpired by the plant is not in balance with that available at the roots, stress results. This imbalance most often results from too-rapid transpiration caused by low humidity, rapid air movement, or both.

More frequent watering, while helpful in such circumstances, cannot entirely overcome this imbalance, and may actually cause a problem by suffocating the roots in sodden medium. Almost all commonly cultivated orchids are accustomed to having some degree of air circulation around their velamen-covered roots. The circulating air is necessary for gas exchange into the root core, which cannot occur if the spongy velamen is kept saturated in a soggy mix. For this reason, the mix in which any given plant is grown must be appropriate to the plant and to the growing area.

Plants with finer roots often need a finer, more water-retentive medium. Plants with coarser roots, which may be accompanied by well-developed water storage organs such as fleshy leaves and stout pseudobulbs, often prefer a coarser medium that dries out more quickly. With some plants, such as vandas and their relatives, the thick fleshy roots actually do best in a basket with no medium whatsoever if sufficient atmospheric moisture—70 percent or greater—can be provided.

As discussed elsewhere, some orchids do best on mounts. Depending on the type, watering may have to be nearly every day, although some will do just fine with less frequent applications of water.

Moisture in the substrate also carries the nutrients needed by the plant in its metabolic processes. When the moisture level is kept too low, the nutrients are not easily available to the plant.

Another factor that profoundly affects watering practices is the quality of the water. In higher rainfall areas, such as the Pacific Northwest and most of the Southeast, water quality will be good, with low dissolved solids and near neutral pH. In the arid Southwest, however, water quality is poor, with a high dissolved solid content and an alkaline

reaction (low pH). Most cultivated orchids originate from areas where the water quality is quite pure. Some are more intolerant of poor quality water than others, with plants from higher elevations and moister environments being especially intolerant of poor-quality water.

Conversely, plants originating in lower moisture areas, such as high in the forest canopy or at the fringes of the forest, may be more tolerant of drying and the subsequent higher salt content of the soil solution. For it is the soil solution—the water in the substrate and the dissolved solids it contains—that is the issue. Both the pH, acid or alkaline reaction, and the salt content—most materials dissolved in soil solution are some sort of salt, which isn't necessarily bad—affect how the plant can take up the necessary nutrients.

Plants grown with good-quality water are free to take up nutrients as needed, while plants grown with poor-quality water are often limited in the amounts they can take up from the substrate. Generally, root systems of plants grown in good-quality water are more robust, as well.

Plants grown with good-quality water are more tolerant of occasional drying. Conversely there is a point beyond which the constant saturation of the medium becomes harmful as well. Many growers find that a reverse osmosis type water purifier is the single best investment they can make in growing good-quality orchids. And, NEVER, ever, use "softened" water, because it is made extra salty by the addition of sodium chloride ($NaCl$, or table salt) to mimic

Left: *Maxillaria speciosa* is grown in a Colombian nursery at 6,000 feet (1,800 meters) and is suitable for cool growing outdoors in the U.S.

soft water. If there is a water softener hooked up for your home use, water from an outside faucet.

## Nutrients

In nature, orchids have a fairly constant supply of nutrients supplied in mild concentrations. Whether growing as epiphytes or as hemi-epiphytic terrestrials in the forest duff, nutrients are available regularly. Epiphytes receive theirs from sources like bird and animal droppings, detritus buildup in their root systems, and by materials dissolved and carried to the roots by rain.

Plants growing in the forest duff have many of the same sources, as well as the gradual breakdown of the duffy leaf litter. What this means to the home grower is that orchids do best with frequent light fertilization, as opposed to periodic heavy applications. The media in which orchids are generally grown affect this, because they are not conducive to nutrient storage over any length of time. Nor are time release fertilizers usually effective, as the coarse nature of most orchid media makes the moisture-regulated release of the contained nutrients irregular.

The mix in which you choose to grow your plants dictates the appropriate fertilizer. Fir-bark-based media require a fertilizer proportionately high in nitrogen to offset the nitrogen robbed by the organisms that break down the bark. Most other commonly used media are best served by a balanced formulation. A brief word here about fertilizer labels is in order. You will always see a formula such as 10-10-10, or 30-10-10, or 0-5-10. This represents the N-P-K formula, or the amounts of available nitrogen (N), phosphorous (P), and potassium (K).

Nitrogen is necessary for plant growth, while phosphorous and potassium are for roots and flowers—this is a gross simplification, but will serve here. Fir-bark-appropriate fertilizers are usually seen as 30-10-10, or 20-10-10, to give the greater amount of nitrogen needed in fir bark. A balanced fertilizer will appear as 10-10-10 or 5-5-5. Another factor to consider is the source for the nitrogen. Generally, nitrogen derived from urea is less available and less desirable than that derived from ammoniacal sources. This is a cost-driven decision on the part of the manufacturer, because urea-based nitrogen is cheaper and more stable than ammoniacal. However, urea-based nitrogen requires the action of soil bacteria active only above 60°Fahrenheit (15°Celsius) to become available

**Above:** The beautiful glossy green color of healthy phalaenopsis leaves.

to the plant. If not converted, it is simply another potentially harmful salt. Ammoniacal nitrogen is readily available to the plant whatever the temperature.

A good general rule of thumb is to fertilize "weakly, weekly." That is, at approximately one-half label strength every week. Every fourth week or so, a thorough watering with clear water will help to keep salt buildup at a minimum. There are several good reasons for the "weakly, weekly" regime. First and foremost, it is best for the plant to have a constant supply of nutrients provided in a mild concentration. Second, it is much easier to remember to fertilize every week than trying to remember did I fertilize last week or not? Third, the more frequent applications will enable the grower to adjust their feedings appropriately to the seasons. As watering tapers off in cooler, darker months, so should fertilizing. Conversely, as water needs increase as the days lengthen, so should fertilization. The observant grower will not only follow the season's dictates in their growing practices, they will note the reactions of their plants and act accordingly.

There are seasonal needs for every orchid plant—light, air, water, and nutrients—and the good grower gets that way by observing their plants' needs throughout the year and meeting them.

# GROWING ORCHIDS AT HOME

*Growing your orchids in the right location is vitally important for their health and increases the likelihood that they will bloom again with the same vigor.*

Home orchid gardeners can grow their plants in such a variety of ways that any starting point is purely arbitrary. The first hurdle to overcome is thinking that orchids are somehow unique in their needs. They are not. They originate, as discussed earlier, in the very same areas as many of our favorite and most time-tested home and garden subjects. And as with any plant, the savvy gardener selects plants based on his or her conditions, coupled with knowledge of what already does well under those conditions. The key is to be an *observant* gardener, to understand plants and how they react to changing conditions. Once the potential orchid grower grasps the concept that orchids are neither unique nor essentially different from plants that they are already growing, success is just a few short steps away.

Most orchid growers start out with either a gift plant from a friend or visitor or with a plant they have purchased on impulse. Thankfully, the single most popular orchid in the world is the moth orchid, *Phalaenopsis*, perhaps because it is also the easiest for home culture, with the longest-lived blooms and the most likely to reflower under home conditions.

A flowering orchid plant can be enjoyed in just about any setting in the home, as long as the area suffers from neither extremes of temperature or excessive dryness. Areas that would be poor choices for orchid display might be next to an unprotected window, by a heat register, or on top of the television. With few exceptions, though, you can place your decorative plant where it is displayed to the highest advantage, both for the plant and for your décor. However, once the plant is finished flowering, it is time to consider where it will be best accommodated to maximize its growth and, hence, its flowering next season.

In the home, most indoor gardeners have already determined appropriate windowsills, or areas near windows, where a variety of their indoor plants do well. The best situations for orchids are east (best), shaded south (next best), or west (adequate). A northern exposure will almost never provide sufficient light to rebloom an orchid and is only useful for orchid plants grown for their foliage, such as jewel orchids. Of course, unless the home has particularly wide windowsills, the grower will have already made accommodation for plants by placing a table or bench next to the window to take advantage of the light. The placement of plants on the bench is one of the first adjustable aspects of indoor culture. This will enable the grower to have a fairly broad range of light regimes available to suit a variety of different orchids. Always remember that the light coming in through your windows will vary with the season.

Perhaps the most difficult aspect of indoor orchid culture is maintaining adequate humidity. Everything in the home—furniture, drapery, heating, and air conditioning—conspires to wick away moisture from the air. Some homeowners have resorted to humidifiers, but these are rarely satisfactory for keeping enough moisture in the air to suit orchids. It is much more practical to create microclimates for your orchid plants. The best way to do this is by grouping plants—not just orchids, but other foliage plants—to take advantage of their collective transpiration. Just this trick alone can often raise humidity to acceptable levels in all but the most desert-like areas. An often-recommended solution is to grow your plants on waterproof trays filled with gravel or stones that are kept

**Right:** A profusion of phalaenopsis make an eye-catching display.

moist. This solution certainly addresses what to do with water that flushes through the plants when you water but has not proven to be very effective for raising humidity to any appreciable amount.

For those gardeners who are able, the single most important aid to good orchid culture is summering their plants outdoors in a sheltered location. First, plants that are grown outdoors during summer months will have the advantage of making most of their seasonal growth under near-natural conditions. This will enable them to flower better and to survive potentially long, cold winters indoors much more effectively.

Second, when plants are moved outdoors in spring, after the danger of frost is past and back indoors in the fall, the grower has two cues to inspect the plants in detail. This close inspection gives the gardener the opportunity to check

for pests and diseases at an early stage and also allows a thorough cleaning of the plants.

It is especially important for the grower to check the plants during the move indoors in fall to ensure that all pests and diseases have been dealt with before the plants are moved indoors to the more crowded winter quarters. Another aspect of successfully utilizing outdoor conditions is to move your plants gradually. Just as you don't spend eight hours at the beach on the first sunny day of spring because you will burn, so will your orchid plants. Move them gradually, over a period of several weeks, into the brighter conditions. Those blessed with nearly frost-free winters can move their plants out well before the Equinox and allow the sun's rising angle in the sky to do the acclimatization job for them. Those further north have to do this task themselves.

Finally, it is imperative that indoor gardeners are observant of the seasonal angle of the sun and how this affects the amount and quality of light entering their windows. As the sun rises higher in the sky, it will be stronger. Conversely, as the sun sinks to a lower angle as the fall season draws nearer, its light will be less powerful. However, except for those lucky enough to have overhead light coming from skylights, all light entering through their windows will be incident, or angled, light, which is intrinsically of lower energy. Plants should be moved further away from the window during brighter months and nearer the window in winter.

## Growing under Lights

Where your home is poorly situated to receive natural light through windows, or in climates where there is a high proportion of gloomy days, the answer may be setting aside an area specifically for growing plants under artificial lights. Many growers supplement their available light with a simple three- or four-tube fluorescent fixture mounted over the plants. This is an excellent way to boost light to your plants without getting too involved with additional expense and complication. If the fixture is mounted 18–24 inches (45–60 cms) over the growing surface, plants requiring more light can be raised closer to the lights by placing them on inverted pots, while those requiring less light can be left at the greater distance.

The advantages of such a setup are manifold: you decide the light intensity and duration; all your plants are concentrated in one area, making watering and inspection for pest or disease problems much easier; and, indeed, pests and diseases are more easily excluded from an in-home growing area. Popular areas of the home for a light garden include an unused bedroom or basement. Wherever you choose to make your plant room, be sure that adequate electricity is available to run the light fixtures as well as

**Left:** Orchid lovers from more northerly climes can boost their range of plants by growing under lights; however, growers need to be careful not to overextend their plants' diurnal range.

timers, heaters, humidifiers, and other equipment. Many growers build special benches for their plants and it is important to add extra insulation to help keep heating and cooling costs to a minimum as well as to be environmentally responsible.

Several other factors to consider for under lights culture are: watering the plants, what to do with water run-off, maintaining adequate humidity, and monitoring of day length. This last point is critical because you will want to replicate seasonal changes so that the plants will have the signals they need to "know" when it is their time to flower. (See page 28 for light exposure levels.) Having the lights on timers is the most popular method of effecting this. Finally, some growers who have an entire room or basement to give over to their plant hobby find that reversing the day and night makes good sense. First, electric rates may be lower for night use. Second, the lights are on when the grower is home from his or her job, when he wants to be working with his plants.

## Growing Outdoors

In mild, frost-free climates, aspiring orchid growers have the opportunity to grow a broad selection of orchids especially adapted for such conditions. The range of orchids available for garden use is ever-expanding, thanks to growers in coastal California and South Florida whose different climates give rise to distinctive offerings.

For those in milder areas exemplified by the Pacific Coast area, available subjects come from higher elevations where light frosts in winter are not uncommon and temperatures remain moderate year round. *Cymbidium, Laelia,* and many members of the *Odontoglossum/Oncidium* group make up just part of this assemblage, which is rounded out by *Zygopetalum* and other showy hybrids and species. All of these types come from the warm summer/cool winter areas whose temperature regime matches that of the Pacific Coast.

The main difference in climate is that the rain tends to come in winter months along the West Coast with colder temperatures, while in their native habitats these plants enjoy their rainfall along with the warmer summer months. If rain can be kept off the plants during the cold months and water provided during warmer months, this group will do very well. Indeed, some plants, such as laelias, will even do well with winter rains, when they seem to undergo a vast proliferation of root growth to take advantage of the available moisture from rain.

Outdoor growers in the Pacific Coast states have some of the same sucking pests, notably aphids, to contend with as indoor growers and have to be especially alert for slugs

**Above:** Jewel orchids such as *Ludisia discolor* offer beautiful foliage even when not in bloom.

and snails, which are endemic to moist gardens. However, with the many effective molluscicides available in bait form, it is simply a matter of using the materials to help keep populations in check.

Growers with warm and wet summer climates, as are found in South Florida and around the Gulf Coast states, do better with more tropical subjects that enjoy the hot, humid summers. These include some of the same subjects that do well on the West Coast, such as cattleyas and many of the oncidiums, while cymbidiums, for the most part, simply will not flower where summers are warm.

However, there is such a broad range of other types, notably from the vanda group that these folks needn't feel short-changed. In these areas where summer rain can often be excessive, measures have to be taken to ensure that plants do not drown as a result of being held in poorly draining media. Many growers in these areas prefer to use mixes based on aggregates or treefern—where they use media at all, because so many plants will do well if simply placed in a slatted wooden basket with no medium, or

placed on a mount. Indeed, many growers actually landscape with select plants, tying them to the tree trunks when the rainy season is due, allowing the naturally occurring moisture to help the plants establish on the trees.

Warm climate outdoor growers have similar pest problems to those on the West Coast but have to be more concerned with disease and fungal problems that flourish under the prevailing humid conditions. Preventative treatments with pesticides or other substances are rarely indicated; however, Florida growers may be forced into periodic applications of fungicides to help keep their collection free of disease. Prevention is easier than cure, and experienced growers make it a regular practice to spray with a fungicide after a prolonged period of heavy rain, such as might accompany a hurricane or tropical storm.

There are many advantages to outdoor growing. The gentle air movement and good-quality light have special qualities that help orchid plants perform well. Old hands can actually tell the difference between a plant grown outdoors or indoors, whether in a greenhouse or in the home. A plant grown outdoors will be stockier and more compact, often with a bronzy tinge to the green of the foliage that results from high light. Plants grown outdoors will tolerate a much higher light regime than those grown under cover. With increased air circulation and higher light, growers will find that more frequent waterings and fertilization will be in order, as well. Outdoor growers may choose to take advantage of naturally occurring shade sources, such as trees, or may wish to construct dedicated shade structures for their plants. A good shade house often looks like a greenhouse without the glazing (glass or fiberglass coating) or it may be as simple as a pipe framework over which shade cloth is tightly strung. An advantage to a dedicated shade structure, particularly in cooler areas where frost may be more severe, is that the structure allows the grower to devise temporary covering for cold spells to help protect the orchids from the worst of the cold. Otherwise, the structures should be open to the elements, which will allow the good air circulation that assists in the production of good plants. And good plants give the best flowers. Indeed, wherever it is possible to grow orchids outdoors, experts prefer it because the plants and flowers are so much healthier and longer lasting.

## Growing under Glass

Sooner or later, almost every serious orchid grower aspires to a greenhouse. A grower who is able to control light, temperature, humidity, and watering is simply able to grow better plants as well as a wider variety. Of course, many simply cannot accommodate a greenhouse structure, for whatever reasons, and they can do very well using some of the techniques described above.

What are the requirements of a good greenhouse? As with the real estate saying, the single most important feature is location, location, location. The best greenhouse sites are where the structure can be oriented north-south along its long axis, well away from any sources of shade such as structures or large trees. The orientation allows the

plants to take advantage of the sun year round as it tracks from higher to lower angles and back again.

Having the long axis run north-south also enables ridge vents that open in a way that is more likely to prevent direct, burning sunlight from entering as it might from an east-west vent setup. Good isolation from shading sources also enables the grower to control the amount and quality of light by adding shade. It is much easier to add shade than to increase light. However, the structure should be relatively convenient to the home or garage for access during poor weather and also because utilities are likely to be more available nearer the home.

The next feature to consider is intimately related to energy needs and temperature control and moderation. Larger internal volumes maintain their temperature better than smaller ones. It is as simple as that. This is even truer with an enclosed structure, because the larger the volume, the lower the surface area to volume ratio will tend to be. And so with a smaller volume, the high surface area will allow more rapid heating or cooling. The bottom line here is that when considering your greenhouse, build a structure that is as large as you can realistically afford. This is not only good sense from a temperature management

**Right:** Once the windowsill is overwhelmed it's time to get serious and invest in a greenhouse, note the overhead fan essential for providing ventilation throughout.

**Above:** In a greenhouse, orchids can be arranged according to their light requirements. The experienced grower makes use of different greenhouse microclimates for growing orchids with specific needs.

standpoint, but because your collection will tend to grow quicker than you could imagine.

Large is good not only in terms of the building's footprint, but also in height. A relatively high greenhouse roof will allow the interior air mass to be larger in proportion to the square footage and provide a useful insulating "cushion" to protect against overheating. All of this has to be sensibly balanced with your ability to manage the heating and cooling facilities for your structure. It is more expensive to artificially heat and cool a larger structure than a smaller one. With modern considerations about energy conservation, most growers have access to a number of solutions for such issues.

Passive heating and cooling is one example. The best greenhouse plans will incorporate both bottom and top vents. This allows for best temperature control without resorting to artificial cooling. In warmer months, both sets

of vents are kept open, allowing the rising warmer air to exit the roof vents, drawing in cooler air through the lower vents. Many different glazing materials exist today. The best have a double-wall construction that takes advantage of the dead air space between the two walls as a means of insulation. This is effective for keeping temperatures down as well as maintaining heat during winter months. Growers with existing structures can emulate double-wall glazing by using bubble-wrap sheeting inside the glass or fiberglass covering. Alternately, a layer of 4- to 6-mil. polyethylene sheeting can be tacked on the inside of structural members to create an insulating space.

For higher structures, especially new ones, growers can opt to have automatically deployed retractable heat blankets installed. Heat blankets are generally strung across the greenhouse at the level of the top of the vertical walls. These open and shut by thermostatic control, helping to trap heat at the lower level where it benefits plants. Heat rises, and if heat can be kept from the upper reaches of the structure where it is more quickly given up to outer, colder air, heating efficiency is much augmented.

Gas-fired space heaters are commonly used. Such heaters may either be suspended high in the greenhouse or at floor level. Either way, fans are used to distribute the warm air. These heaters, while economical to buy and install, are not always the best answer because they can be quite drying and occasionally leak damaging pollutants into the greenhouse. Savvy growers opt for under-bench heating systems when they are able. While such systems are more costly to install initially, their increased effectiveness and efficiency offer a quick payback. This method of heating is accomplished by installing finned tubing under the benches. The tubing is fed by either a water heater or a steam boiler. The system radiates heat to the plants' root zones. This not only heats the plants more effectively, less heat is lost to the surrounding atmosphere. Finally, plants grown with bottom heat just seem to do better.

In the same way that light and heat are related, so are heat and humidity. As discussed earlier, as heat rises, so

**Below:** Orchids are pollinated by placing the pollinia from one flower on to the stigmatic surface of another. Once established in the hobby, the chance to create a new hybrid often proves an irresistible challenge.

should humidity and, conversely, as temperatures fall, so should the humidity. A greenhouse, which encloses a fixed volume of air, must have moisture added as temperatures rise to compensate for the lowering relative humidity. Modern greenhouses can have installed under-bench misting systems actuated by humidistats. It is critical that the misting system be under the bench so that the water does not get on the plants unnecessarily. If water stands on the plants, it provides an avenue for the entry of diseases, as well as being a potential source of the buildup of unsightly mineral deposits.

Well-ventilated greenhouses will see the humidity naturally begin to fall as the day goes on toward night, and experienced growers allow this to happen, because the plants prefer it. If your greenhouse does not have an automatic humidity system, you will need to add humidity manually by damping down the walks and under-bench areas with a hose. A humidity gauge, available through greenhouse suppliers, is an indispensable tool for this monitoring activity. Fans, placed at various levels throughout the greenhouse, will keep the air moving and fresh and spread humidity evenly throughout the space.

Greenhouse plant benches should allow water to drain freely yet be resistant to moisture-related rot or other damage. For this reason, most benching is at least partly of metal construction, generally from varying gauges of wire mesh strung on either metal or wood support framing. The bench framing needs to be strong to support the weight of the plants and pots. Most growers prefer their benches to be at a height convenient for reaching across, as well as a width—usually no more than 60 inches (150 cms) if free standing—that allows easy access to the plants.

Some growers like to put another layer of benching around the greenhouse perimeter, about 18 inches (45 cms) or so above the first and only half as wide. This allows for accommodation of substantially more plants without interfering with the light and watering requirements of the bottom layer. Another method of increasing plant holding capacity is to raise some plants up on inverted pots. It is important to maintain proper spacing on the benches to promote good air circulation and allow the grower to

**Below:** A colorful display of showy miltoniopsis hybrids in the home greenhouse.

visually inspect every plant. Finally, placing plants together by type and size will allow ease of watering.

There are a variety of ways to provide proper light levels in the greenhouse. These include simply painting the glass with a water-based latex paint, to applying varying weights of shade cloth, to installing specially-tinted glazing. In more northerly areas, shade that can be varied according to season is a cost-effective investment. More southern areas can get away with the same degree of shade the year round, because the light intensity varies less the further south one lives. Perhaps the most effective method of shading—one that also serves as an insulating feature by trapping a layer of dead air between the shading material and the glazing—is to suspend shade cloth about 18 inches (45 cms) above the glazing on an external frame. When differing light levels are desired within a smaller structure, cheesecloth, or similar material, can be tacked inside the primary shading material to provide an additional layer of gentle, diffuse shade.

In the end, growing orchids in a greenhouse represents the pinnacle of the hobby. The potential results are well worth the effort. But the potential pitfalls are many. If the conditions are too crowded, if the grower is insufficiently observant, if problems are allowed to fester without relief, if potting is not kept up, if diseased plants are allowed into the collection, if, if, if …

# BASIC TOOLS AND EQUIPMENT

*Few expensive tools are needed for orchids, but growers will need to spend their time—not their money—making sure they have the correct medium and container to match to the orchid.*

**Pots:** There are many types of pots available that are suited for the culture of orchids but the basic choice remains: clay or plastic. Most clay orchid pots are terra-cotta and often have additional drainage either as holes or slots around the bottom edge of the pot. There are several individuals offering clay orchid pots that are decorative as well as functional, and you may find these worth investigating.

The basic characteristics of an orchid pot are that it is shallow in relation to its height and has additional holes for drainage and root aeration. Plastic pots generally have the same features, but the plastic retains moisture longer than a porous clay pot. Additionally, plastic pots require specific rhizome clips and stakes that don't always anchor as well as their clay counterparts. In either case, it is important to choose the type of pot based upon your other cultural factors, such as average temperature, air movement, frequency of watering, and choice of potting medium as well as the genera being grown.

Generally, temperate growers who have greenhouses tend to prefer plastic pots and a moisture-retentive mix such as fir bark or sphagnum. Subtropical growers, whose plants are exposed to the elements, tend to use fast-draining media, such as the aggregates and clay pots. Subtropical

growers, who also often grow their plants outdoors or in areas exposed to the wind, find that clay pots give a weighted, bottom-heavy aspect that does not blow over as easily as plastic.

Both clay and plastic pots are available in a wide range of sizes from 2 inches (5 cms) up to 12 inches (30 cms) and larger. Choose the appropriate size to allow for approximately two years' growth.

**Drainage:** Whether or not to use additional drainage material in the bottom of orchid pots is a continuing debate. Many growers advocate putting some sort of drainage material in the bottom, whereas others prefer to fill the whole pot with medium. Although the choice is ultimately yours, most recommend that you use drainage. The argument against additional drainage material is that it doesn't really serve any useful purpose, and that it only provides a good hiding place for pests such as slugs and snails. If you regularly bait for these pests, this is not an issue.

The purpose of putting pieces of broken crock in the bottom of orchid pots is to prevent the medium from compacting and blocking the drainage holes. It also serves

Clay pots

Plastic pots

Fine fir bark

Coarse fir bark

the purpose of providing aeration to the interior of the pot where stagnant conditions easily develop. Indeed, certain pot manufacturers have created pots with drainage built in as upside-down slotted cones. This consideration is more critical as pot size increases and becomes imperative when growing specimen-size plants. Without drainage, the center of the medium in a 12-inch pot can become very dank.

Any coarse, inert, inorganic material can be used as drainage. Broken clay pots (sterilized), styrofoam, and landscape lava rock are all good choices and are easily available. Lighter materials can help reduce the weight of large specimen plants, while smooth river rock can add stability to a top-heavy phalaenopsis or dendrobium in a plastic pot. The most important qualities are that the material is coarse enough to provide adequate air space and not break down in the pot.

### Potting Media

**Fir bark:** Today, sterilized fir bark is probably the most commonly used orchid potting material. Its ease of use and comparatively low cost make it an excellent choice for growing orchids of most genera. Sterilized fir bark comes from several species of western U.S. trees including white fir and Douglas fir. It is cleaned and graded before being offered for sale as a potting medium. Fine grades are

suitable for seedlings, whereas coarser grades—pieces up to 1-1/2 inches (2–3 cms) may be used for large pots. As with other materials, fir bark may be enhanced with additives, such as perlite, charcoal, aggregates, or redwood chips. These are often sold as proprietary bagged mixes.

Potting orchids with fir bark is easier than potting in most other media; the relatively uniform pieces readily fall into place among the orchid roots. Because fir bark may be resistant to water at first, many growers prefer to soak it before use. This also serves to remove some of the dust generated in shipping, which will sink to the bottom.

Bacteria that feed on the bark and bring about its eventual decay use considerable available nitrogen, which may leave orchids nutritionally deficient. Therefore, it is necessary to use a high-nitrogen fertilizer, such as 30-10-10 for orchids grown in fir bark.

In a controlled environment, fir bark may last two years in a pot. It has a tendency to break down much quicker in warm subtropical conditions and therefore is not used in these areas as frequently as tree fern or aggregates.

**Tree fern:** Also known by its Hawaiian name hapuu, it is the fibrous trunk of various species of tropical tree ferns. It is available as logs, slabs, or other solid shapes that may be used to mount orchids directly. It is also available in

Charcoal

Perlite

Aliflor

Lava Rock

shredded form in several grades of coarseness. Chunks of tree fern may also be found at times and they are useful for larger pots and specimen plants. Fine tree fern may be used alone or mixed with other ingredients for compots and seedlings.

Tree fern has excellent properties as an orchid-potting medium; it is easy to use and provides good drainage and aeration to roots. However, growers with tender hands may want to use gloves when potting with tree fern, because it can be abrasive. It provides minimal nutrition to plants and lasts about two years under normal growing conditions.

Occasionally, tree fern is mixed with additives such as redwood bark, which is thought to discourage snow mold. Coarse aggregates can also be mixed in to "stretch" the tree fern and improve drainage. Orchids grown in tree fern are best fertilized with a balanced fertilizer, i.e. 20-20-20.

*Dicksoniaceae* and *Cyatheaceae* tree fern species are listed on Appendix II of CITES—an international treaty first drawn up in 1973 to prevent the over-exploitation of wildlife resources. They are endangered in many of their native habitats. Other alternatives may be easier to find and more ecologically sound. Ask your provider about the source of the tree fern material he sells. Support those who practice sustainable use of forest resources.

**Aggregates:** The term aggregates refers to non-organic media such as lava rock and gravel. For the sake of convenience, we include expanded mineral products such as Aliflor and Solite as well as mined products such as Australian diatomite. Like other potting media, these materials are available graded by size, with the smaller sizes being used for seedlings and miniatures and the larger sizes being used for specimen plants and large pots. The larger sizes are also useful as drainage for other potting media.

Being inorganic, these materials do not break down and are ideally suited for warm climates and outdoor growing in rainy areas. Heavier aggregates, in concert with clay pots, can provide the firm footing needed by top-heavy orchids in windy tropical areas. Their quick drainage also allows orchids to withstand considerable rain during wet summer months.

Aggregates are easy to use; the uniform pieces readily fall into place among the orchid roots. Keep in mind that large pots tend to get heavy, especially if the pot is clay. Although Solite is reported to hold up to 30 percent of its weight in water, these materials generally require more frequent watering than organic media. As with other media, additives such as sphagnum may be used to modify the moisture-holding properties. Aggregates provide excellent drainage and aeration to orchid root systems and will last indefinitely. Although they can be reused, this is not advisable unless the used media can be sterilized in a kiln.

Complete nutrition must be supplied when potting with aggregates; use a balanced fertilizer such as 20-20-20. It is also recommended to thoroughly flush potted orchids with clean water monthly to avoid fertilizer salts from building up. Many growers like to prerinse their medium prior to use to remove dust and fine debris.

**Sphagnum moss:** This has become increasingly popular as an orchid-potting medium in recent years, particularly with the introduction of high-quality, long-fibered New Zealand sphagnum. Comparable quality is also available from select Chilean sources. There are different grades of sphagnum available from locations throughout the world; choose the one that fits your budget and quality requirements.

Sphagnum is easy to pot with; however, you should presoak it overnight in a bucket of warm water. Many growers

Osmunda

Coconut Husk Chips

like to add a teaspoon of an algicide such as Physan or RD-20. Squeeze it out gently before packing it around the roots, taking care to not pack too tightly. A rhizome clip or stake may be used to stabilize the orchid.

Sphagnum moss is difficult to rewet once it has dried out so it is best to keep the plants evenly moist but not soaking! Adjust your watering schedule accordingly. As a result, this medium is not for orchids that like to dry thoroughly between waterings.

Although it is thought that the moss supplies some minor nutrition, it is best to fertilize plants potted in sphagnum with a balanced fertilizer such as 20-20-20. Additives such as charcoal and perlite are often used to prevent the moss from compacting and keep the mix open. Sphagnum can last up to two years but in practice, plants are usually repotted yearly, especially phals.

Sphagnum moss can harbor the fungus that causes the lymph infection *Sporotrichosis*. Although cases of infection are not especially common among orchid growers, the fungus can enter the body through a cut or other opening and cause symptoms from mild to severe. As a precaution, wear rubber gloves when working with sphagnum moss.

**Osmunda:** Until the early 1950s, osmunda was the potting medium used for growing orchids. Its increasing scarcity and consequently high price has caused it to fall out of favor. It also requires some skill to be able to successfully pot with osmunda. Other potting materials available today are much easier to use. There are certain instances when this medium might be just what is called for to coax a recalcitrant orchid into growth. It is also useful to put a small pad of osmunda beneath the rhizome when attaching a plant to a mount; this provides a little extra moisture while the plant gets established.

The fibrous roots of the osmunda fern provide a higher quantity of nutrients than most other potting materials, therefore they require more dilute fertilizer application. Use one-half the strength used for other media. Despite the fine texture of osmunda, it does not break down quickly and will generally last in excess of two years. Additives such as charcoal can be used to maintain the openness of the mix and keep it from souring.

Potting with osmunda requires some practice; chunks are torn into appropriately sized pieces and forced into the pot and around the roots with a "potting stick" or similar tool, creating enough pressure against the roots to hold the orchid firmly in place. An orchid that has been properly potted in osmunda usually requires no clips or stakes unless it is top-heavy by nature.

**Coconut husk chips (CHC):** Graded chips, or chunks of coconut husk have enjoyed some popularity as an orchid growing medium. Indications are that it may offer better aeration and stay less wet than coconut fiber. Some growers have had success using the fine grade on its own as a seedling medium. It seems to provide a constant, even source of moisture without the dry-to-wet problems of sphagnum, yet does not stay soggy. It is common practice with this medium to provide an overnight soaking prior to rinsing with water to leach out any accumulated salts that may be present on the coconut husk, depending on its source. The chunks may be used on their own or mixed with charcoal, Aliflor, or lava rock.

There are also many formulated potting mixes available at garden supply stores that are suitable for growing a wide range of orchids. We have not included those here because we do not endorse any particular proprietary potting mix and the types and availability vary regionally.

**Mounts:** Although most orchids may be successfully grown in pots, certain species prefer to be mounted on a substrate more closely resembling the one they would grow on in nature. The basic requirements of a mounting material are much the same as a potting material; it must drain perfectly and not decompose rapidly.

**Cork plaque**

The most commonly available mounting materials are slabs or logs of tree fern, cork bark, or cypress. Occasionally, one can find pieces of Florida buttonwood or other hardwoods that make good mounting materials. Tree fern is the most moisture-retentive of the three and may also be found carved into decorative shapes and totems. These materials may be purchased in large sizes and sawed to meet individual requirements or purchased in assorted sizes.

Any hardwood that is nonresinous and does not decay rapidly can probably be used for mounting orchids. Inquire locally to see what local materials other growers might use. When using tree fern mounts, be sure to orient them so that the fibers are going up and down in order to provide proper drainage.

**Baskets:** A very convenient way to grow orchids is to use baskets. Often, the plant won't need to be repotted until the basket deteriorates. If the plant begins to outgrow its home, it can simply be placed, basket and all, in a larger basket. These containers, because of their open nature, also have the advantage of being better able to meet epiphytic orchids' drainage and root aeration requirements. Some orchids, notably those in the *Vanda* group, prefer to be grown in baskets because of their rambling aerial roots. Indeed, most growers in subtropical areas of Florida and the Gulf States use no medium at all when growing vandaceous plants in baskets.

Wire or plastic baskets are available, but wooden baskets are the most commonly used. They range in size from 4 to 16 inches (10–40 cms) and are usually square but can be hexagonal. Cedar and teak are the most common woods and cypress baskets are available from time to time. Teak baskets tend to last longer and consequently are more expensive. When using a fine potting medium in a basket, line it first with an old piece of fiberglass window screen, sphagnum moss, or coconut fiber to keep the medium from falling out.

The main disadvantage of baskets is that they must be hung. Also, the display of blooming plants is not as easy as with a pot. Wide-ranging roots may also be a problem, preventing easy placement in containers for the home.

**Wire products:** Wire is used to fasten, secure, stabilize, and hang orchids. Although it is easy to make your own, it is more convenient to buy premade wire products. Rhizome clips are the most straightforward way to stabilize a newly potted sympodial orchid. Styles are available for both plastic and clay pots. You have passed the potting test when you can secure a mature cattleya with one properly placed rhizome clip. Occasionally, a tall plant needs a little extra support. The grower can use a straight stake that fastens to the edge of the pot for this purpose.

A ring stake, or hoop, will help contain an unruly orchid as well as provide support. Single and double pot hangers in an assortment of lengths allow you to place a pot almost anywhere. Many growers hang their whole collection using "s" hooks of varying lengths to achieve intermediate heights. Baskets are hung with three or four strands of light-gauge wire. Fourteen or 17-gauge wire is useful for attaching plants to mounts or engineering a vanda into a basket.

**Stakes:** Bamboo and other straight stakes may be inserted into the potting medium to provide additional support for a newly-potted orchid. They are also used for setting a vandaceous plant into a basket. Their primary use is to support the inflorescence of an orchid in a more attractive fashion as well as prevent its collapse or breakage.

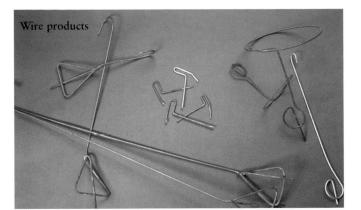

Wire products

Bamboo stakes

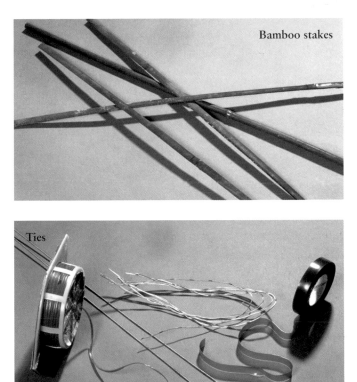

Ties

**Ties:** Like wire products, ties are essential ancillary items to orchid growing and potting. Many growers like to tie pseudobulbs together to make a neater arrangement when repotting. Some may tie a plant to a support stake to add additional security. Plants can be tied to mounts using almost any material including monofilament fishing line or old pantyhose cut into strips. A basic selection of ties includes plastic ribbon tie, twist tie, bell wire, and perhaps, some monofilament or twine.

**Name tags:** Help eliminate nameless orchids; always use a name tag. There are labels available in a style to suit almost any use, so keep a selection on hand. Most are plastic; aluminum tags are available for extreme growing

**Name tag**

**Fungicide**

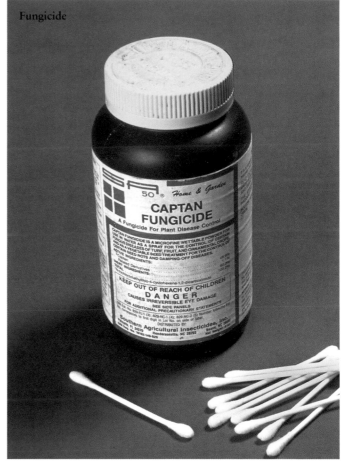

conditions or where permanency is desired. Some provide spaces for bloom and repot information; some are available in colors so that you may code certain plants. Most simply slip into the pot, while others tie on with wire or loops.

**Fungicide:** A wettable fungicide powder should be used to dress freshly cut plant parts. This provides a barrier to infection until the orchid heals itself. An inexpensive product such as Captan, Ferbam, or Zineb can be made into a paste about the consistency of heavy cream and dabbed onto the cut part using disposable cotton swabs. Some growers prefer to just dab a little of the powder onto freshly cut orchid tissue. Fungicide can also be mixed in a quart hand sprayer according to label instructions and used for spraying seedlings or plants that have been bruised during unpotting.

## Tools

**Leverage:** A grower doesn't need to buy a leverage tool. It is easy to appropriate something to use for this simplest and most primitive of all tools. It is used for prying orchids

out of pots. Any sturdy piece of metal will do the job. It should be sharp enough to work between the pot and the medium but not so sharp as to maim you if you slip. There are times when you may need to apply considerable force, such as when repotting a cattleya overdue for dividing. A dull wood chisel works quite well, as does a dull kitchen knife with a stiff blade, but buy one for this specific use because you'll ruin kitchen utensils. You may be able to find special tools that have features that are useful to the orchid grower, such as serrations at garden supply centers and in catalogs. Look around, and find tools that are comfortable for you.

**Shears and clippers:** Garden shears are indispensable to orchid growers. Their most important use is during repotting to trim old roots and dead leaves, and also perform a general cleanup of the plant. Shears come in a variety of different styles but usually have either straight needle-nose blades or curved blades. The straight blades are perfect for getting into tight areas to cut away old roots, whereas the curved blades will cut through thick rhizomes more easily. It's a good idea to have several styles on the potting bench.

Having several pairs also allows you to continue working without having to stop between each plant to sterilize tools. Although stainless-steel shears are a luxury, constantly sterilizing them on a flame can ruin the temper as well as the rust resistance. It is a better idea to buy a number of inexpensive tools that can be renewed every few years. A pair of utility scissors is also useful to cut thin leaves and roots during a potting session.

**Torch:** There are other methods to sterilize potting tools, but a propane torch is by far the most effective, as well as convenient. It's hard to spot virus-affected plants in the early stages and your orchids may look disease-free, but you only have to cut one virused plant to spread the disease throughout your whole collection. Experienced orchid growers sterilize their cutting tools between each and every plant. Passing a blade through the flame for few moments on each side is sufficient to kill any virus.

A propane torch with automatic ignition will save you a lot of time and frustration and is a cost effective investment. The fuel cylinders themselves are inexpensive. If you feel uncomfortable using a torch, other options might be an alcohol lamp or soaking the tools in a saturated solution of TSP (trisodium phosphate). Although the latter technique has gone in and out of popularity, it is generally impractical because tools must soak for an extended period of time to kill viruses with any degree of certainty.

**Pliers and cutters:** It's a good idea to keep a couple pair of pliers and wire cutters at hand during a potting session because there's always something that needs to be bent, twisted, cut, or removed. Lineman's pliers are a multipurpose tool for the orchid grower; they can cut through wire hangers with relative ease or bend a rhizome clip to make it fit tighter. Their substantial weight allows them to be used as a sort of hammer. The angular jaws can enlarge the drainage holes in clay pots with ease or force a tight stake into position. Diagonal cutters can be used to cut lighter gauges of wire used for hanging baskets.

**Knives:** Every potting bench should have a knife or two. A sharpened putty knife may be just the right tool for

**Shears and Clippers**

loosening roots from the outside of a clay pot. An old kitchen knife or pocketknife can also be very useful. Look for a blade that is fairly stiff and five or six inches (13–15 cms) long. Always take care when using knives, do not use them as levers and do not use excessive force.

**Toothbrush and alcohol:** Repotting an orchid is the best opportunity to perform a thorough inspection and detect any problems that may have gone unnoticed. Insects often like to hide under the protective sheaths covering the pseudobulbs and rhizomes.

An old toothbrush dipped in a little rubbing alcohol will do an excellent job of removing dried sheaths. In doing so, you may also kill any insect pests that may be present. Always use care when scrubbing around new leads and root tips, these parts are very fragile and damage can set the plant back.

**Pliers and wire cutters**

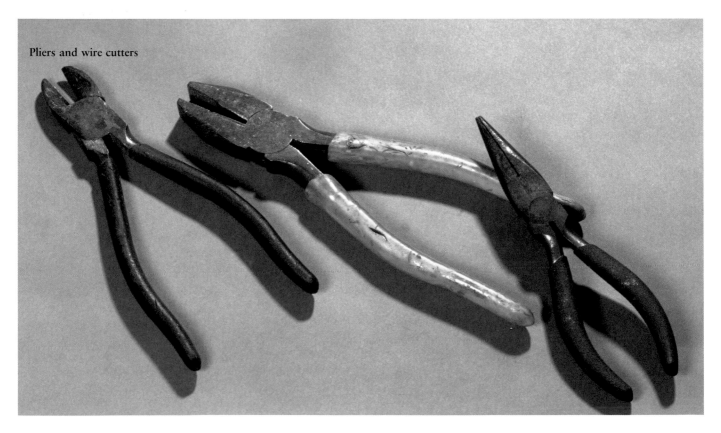

There are other tools that may help you with your orchid potting—you are sure to add some of your own as you gain experience.

- An electric or cordless drill and an assortment of different drill bits make securing a vandaceous orchid in a basket easy work. A drill is also useful for drilling holes in mounts for hangers.

- A wooden dowel of 1 to 1-1/2 inches (2–4 cms) diameter can be used as a potting stick with certain media. A wooden hammer handle will also do the job.

- Have a lot of orchids to mount? A hot glue gun makes mounting small orchids fast and easy.

- Tweezers can be helpful in removing small weeds from orchid pots or stripping away a remnant of dried sheath. Be extremely careful around the tender new leads and root tips. They are also handy for removing broken glass when deflasking.

- Inexpensive plastic buckets and storage containers are always useful to orchid growers for soaking potting medium or creating a special mix.

- A 12–16 inches (30–40 cms) metal rod can be used for knocking out the bottom of flasks. You can buy a piece of threaded rod or metal stock at home centers and cut to a convenient length. A round file may also work.

- Scraps of fiberglass window screen can be used to line baskets to prevent the medium from falling out. Small strips can be used to fasten an orchid to a mount.

- Aluminum oven trays in various sizes are handy to keep on hand for deflasking. They can also be filled with gravel and used as humidity trays for small orchids or compots (orchids from "community pots") that have been recently repotted.

- A pair of bolt cutters can be useful for removing wire hangers from around fragile new growth. Although they can be heavy and awkward to use, the smallest ones you can find should do just fine for cutting 10- or 12-gauge galvanized wire.

- Vinyl gutter guard is a multi-purpose item that belongs on the potting bench. Available in rolls, convenient lengths can be cut to secure pads of sphagnum to mounts. You can even fashion it into custom net pots.

**Razor blades:** Disposable, single-edge razor blades are an easy way to maintain sanitation when potting; use them once and discard. They provide a low-cost and quicker alternative to repeatedly sterilizing a knife. Some growers keep an old coffee can handy, putting used blades into the can. The used blades can be sterilized in the oven at 350° Fahrenheit (175° Celsius) for 20 minutes or so. The blades may give several uses this way and will give a nice clean cut.

Use razor blades with extreme care and limit their use to cutting nothing thicker than a thin leaf, which they often do better than shears. A rhizome is too thick, too tough, and too dangerous to attempt cutting with a razor blade; shears are much safer. Also, be sure to keep razor blades out of the reach of children and dispose of them properly.

**Potting demonstrations**

Armed with this comprehensive set of tools, some spare pots, and the perfect potting mix, orchid enthusiasts can apply themselves to the essential task of potting, mounting or remounting their orchids. This process will always be necessary, as healthy plants will grow beyond the size of their original container and potting media need frequent changes. However, with some orchid families, overpotting, i.e. giving an orchid too much space too soon, is worse than leaving it with too little.

On the following pages you will find out how to mount an orchid for a hanging display; gluemount an orchid; repot and divide a cymbidium; and repot cattleyas, dendrobiums, oncidiums, paphiopedilums, phalaenopsis and vandaceous orchids.

# MOUNTING ORCHIDS FOR A HANGING DISPLAY

*Many orchids are epiphytes, living their lives rooted high in the branches or on the trunk of a host tree. Orchid growers can exploit this ability and create stunning hanging displays by transferring plants, such as cattleyas or epidendrums, to a wood or bark mount and liberating them from their earthbound pot.*

**2** As always, sterilize your cutting tools by passing them through the flame for a couple of minutes. Remember to resterilize before cutting another plant.

**1** Here is a seedling of *Cattleya walkeriana*, a species noted for its rambling growth that is perfectly suited for growing on a mount and being liberated from this crusty old pot.

**3** Remove the seedling from the pot using a lever if needed. If you have trouble removing the plant, sacrifice the pot by breaking it if it is clay or cutting with shears if it is plastic. Remove any old, decaying potting medium.

## Basic Repotting Rules

- When dividing, only propagate vigorous, free-flowering stock; there is little merit in producing additional stock of orchids that are unsatisfactory.

- Always sterilize cutting tools between cutting plants by passing the tool through a flame for a few moments on each side.

- Cut surfaces of live plant tissue should be dressed with a broad-spectrum fungicide, as a powder or mixed into a paste, to prevent infection. Use disposable cotton swabs.

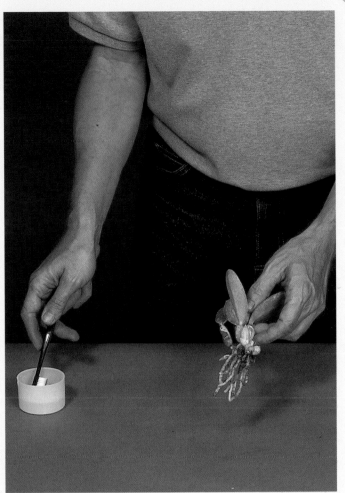

**4** Trim away any old, untidy dead roots or long, dead flower spikes.

**5** An old toothbrush dipped in rubbing alcohol is useful for removing old sheaths and eliminating any pests that may be present. Be very careful not to damage the new growth or root tips when scrubbing the pseudobulbs.

**6** Use a drill and an appropriate bit to drill a centered hole near one end of the mount. Here we are using a cypress slab, but cork bark is another favorite material. Hardwoods that are nonresinous and will not deteriorate quickly may be suitable mounts.

**7** With a pair of pliers, fashion a short piece of 12- or 14-gauge galvanized wire into an S-shaped hanger.

**8** A little wad of dampened sphagnum or osmunda can provide additional moisture while the plant gets established.

**9** Place the orchid near the bottom so that the newest growth is facing the top of the mount.

**10** Use plastic-coated twist-tie material, wire, or monofilament fishing line to fasten the orchid to the piece of cypress. Some growers use strips of old pantyhose to fasten delicate plants. The orchid must be anchored firmly in order for it to establish itself on the mount.

**11** Here is what a finished mounted orchid should look like. Plants can grow on mounts until they either outgrow the space or the mount deteriorates.

*Cattleya walkeriana* comes into bloom once more after being successfully mounted.

# GLUE MOUNTING SMALL ORCHIDS

*Many orchids, such as those in the* Maxillaria *family, are climbers. They also have long rhizomes as do bulbophyllums, brassavolas, and Brazilian Miltonias* species. *They are all suitable for rooting on a mount.*

**1** This maxillaria is well suited to growing on a mount because of the long rhizomes. Other plants with long rhizomes between bulbs that are good candidates for mount culture are many bulbophyllums, brassavolas, and Brazilian Miltonias. Plants that need to be thoroughly dried between waterings, or are denizens of the bright fringes of the forest canopy, such as *Cattleya walkeriana,* are also best on mounts. Green tips on the wiry roots indicate that this is a good time to repot this orchid.

**2** Remove the orchid from the pot, and clean away the old potting medium. Remove any dead roots, sheaths, or old flower spikes. Inspect the plant for any disease or insect problems, and treat as required. You may use an old toothbrush and rubbing alcohol to carefully scrub away old sheaths. This is also a good time to examine the plant's growth habits. Some plants will have a climbing habit, such as this maxillaria, and are best suited to a vertical mount.

**3** Make a hole for a hanger using an electric or portable drill. Insert a piece of 10- or 12-gauge galvanized wire through the hole and fashion into an "S."

**4** Examine the cork slab for any natural crevasses that may anchor the orchid more securely. Test fit the orchid on the slab, making note of where you will actually place it.

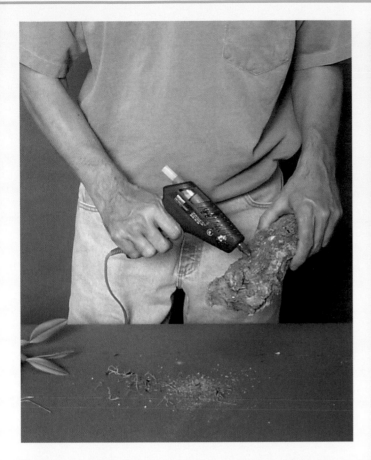

5 Squeeze a few dabs of glue onto the contact points of where you will attach the orchid. Place the orchid on the mount, and hold in place for a few moments until the glue sets. Although the glue is not that hot, it is better to apply it to the mount rather than risk possible damage to tender plant tissue. Remember that you are attempting to not only mount the plant so that it will grow best, but so that it will give a natural appearance. These two goals are often the same. The rhizome should be against the mounting surface and the lead growth should be toward the top of the mount.

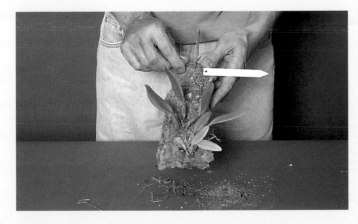

6 Attach a name tag. You're done! A hot glue gun is an efficient way to quickly mount orchids.

**Above:** A stunning *Epidendrum parkinsonianum* shows the pendant habit of the plant, which is growing on a bark mount.

# REPOTTING AND DIVIDING CYMBIDIUMS

*Cymbidiums are a family of large orchids that can soon overwhelm a small pot. They can easily be divided into smaller plants, and the process of division gives the grower an opportunity to prune off dead roots and refresh the plant media. The result is two healthy vigorous plants where before there was one.*

**1** A healthy cymbidium will have a dense root mass. This plant was growing in a plastic nursery pot. We have cut the pot with shears, and will peel it away to free the plant. Many times the roots will so completely fill the pot that no old medium is apparent.

**2** As always, sterilize your cutting tools before cutting any plant tissue, and resterilize between plants. Here, the grower is using a torch to sterilize his cutting tool. This is the surest way of disinfecting the tool of virus.

**3** Now is the time to clean up the plant by cutting off any dead or unhealthy leaves or leaf tips. Cutting the leaves at an angle will give a more natural appearance.

**4** Although we could make several plants from this overgrown cymbidium, we will divide it into two large pieces. Notice that there seems to be a natural division in the middle of the plant.

5 Because of the dense root mass, shears are of little use at this point. We are using a special potting tool with a dull serrated blade to cut through the root mass. A knife or small saw will also do the job. When using a knife, you may need to exert some force to cut through the thick cymbidium roots. You may find it useful to cut an inch or so off the bottom of the root mass as a good starting point. This will give you access to the interior of the root mass where you will more easily find natural division points.

**Be extremely careful!** Always cut away from your hands.

6 It may not be necessary to cut all the way through the root mass. Once you have cut partially through, you should be able to pull the pieces apart. The roots can often be separated with a little extra effort. If this is not possible, you will need to cut deeper.

7 Now we have two divisions, and can finish cleaning them up for potting. Remove the old potting medium and any dead roots that easily pull away. Also, remove any old leaf sheaths around the bulbs.

8 Trim away any soft, mushy, dead roots with sterile shears. If the roots are basically in good condition, you do not need to be too extreme. The more roots you leave, the better the plant will be anchored.

**9** Select a pot that will allow for about two years of growth. As a general rule, cymbidiums are potted in plastic pots.

**10** We will use a fir bark mix that contains charcoal, perlite, and Aliflor. Straight medium-grade fir bark is also a good choice. Presoaking fir bark will allow it to absorb water more readily.

**11** Place a layer of fir bark mix in the bottom of the pot. You do not need to use any drainage material. If you wish, you can add a few large landscape river rocks that will make the pot more stable and not so top-heavy when the plant is in flower.

**12** Place the plant in the pot, and begin adding media all around the root mass until it is within a half an inch of the rim of the pot. Do not cover the base of the pseudobulbs! Gently tapping the pot on the potting surface will help to settle the medium in and around the roots.

13 One long-time technique for potting cymbidiums involves using a wooden dowel as a potting stick. The tool is used to compact the fir bark around the root mass to secure the plant firmly. Do not pound on the medium. It is a tamping movement to help firm up the plant with the mix incorporated around the roots. Firm is the watchword.

14 This method does a good job of securing the plant without the use of any additional hardware.

15 A firmly-anchored orchid ensures it will quickly establish in its new pot. You can test the anchoring by suspending the plant from a group of leaves and looking to see if the pot slips.

16 Prepare a name tag and insert it into the pot. Most growers like to put the date of potting on the name tag to aid their memory about when the plant next needs potting and in what month best results were obtained.

# Repotting Cattleya with Styrofoam Peanuts

*Styrofoam peanuts make an excellent additive for orchid potting when used as drainage in the bottom of the pot. They also allow the grower to use less fir bark. Do not use water soluble peanuts, which are generally green in color. If in doubt, soak a few in a bowl of water for a half hour.*

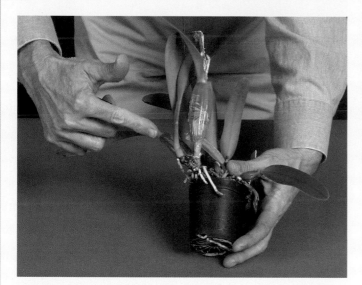

1 The best time to repot a cattleya is when a cluster of healthy green root tips appear at the base of a lead. This signifies the start of a growth cycle, and the plant will quickly establish itself in a pot of new medium. New root tips can appear at varying times in the development of a new growth, so it is important to pay attention to your plant so that you can repot at the proper time to ensure success. This is a good reason to write the potting date on the plants' name tags as a reminder.

2 It is a good idea to begin potting each plant by sterilizing your tools. Sterilized tools will not spread disease and virus from plant to plant. Although there are other techniques, a torch is the surest and quickest. Run both sides of the tool through the flame for a minute, until red hot.

3 This cattleya seedling was potted in a plastic pot. Removal is easy. Squeeze the pot all around until the roots are loosened from the sides of the pot. If necessary, use a dull tool, such as an oyster knife, to leverage the orchid out of the pot.

**4** Begin working the old potting medium away from the roots with your fingers. The oyster knife can also be used. Partially closed shears used in a twisting fashion do a good job of removing dead roots and old media. If you have access to an outside hose, a jet of water will do a good final cleanup of removing the old medium. The idea is to remove as much medium as possible without damaging any live, healthy roots.

**5** Cut away any dead roots with a sterilized cutting tool. Dead roots will appear soft and mushy or dry and papery. If the velamen—the soft white spongy root covering—is gone, leaving only a thin root core with the appearance of a wire, cut it off. A good rule of thumb is to remove old roots to a length that is about 2/3 of the depth of the pot into which the plant will be moved. This allows them to serve as good anchorage, while not leaving excess injured plant tissue that can lead to rot.

**6** To fit the orchid into a reasonably sized pot, and also because they serve little function, remove old back-bulbs. In this case, we will remove the small seedling-growth pseudobulbs. When you are removing old pseudobulbs or if you are dividing a plant, be sure to keep at least four to five good, live pseudobulbs per division.

7 This is a good time to give the orchid a general cleanup. Cut away any old bloom spikes. Use a toothbrush dipped in rubbing alcohol to gently scrub away dried sheaths. Inspect for any signs of pests or disease, and treat appropriately. The rubbing alcohol will eliminate some soft-bodied pests.

8 Mix a little broad spectrum fungicide powder with a little water to make a liquid the consistency of heavy cream. A 35mm film can makes good storage and keeps it ready for next use. Using a disposable cotton swab, dab a little fungicide powder on the cut rhizome to prevent infection.

9 Here is our unpotted, cleaned-up cattleya, ready to repot.

10 These are the materials we will use to pot the orchid in its new home (left to right): fir-bark mix, styrofoam peanuts, clean clay pots, rhizome clips, name tags, and a cleaned-up orchid. It is a good idea to presoak fir bark for an hour before use to improve its water-absorption qualities and remove excess dust. If using coconut husk chips, buy them pre-washed to avoid salt contamination.

11 Select a pot that will allow for about two-years growth. Use a plastic or clay container, depending on your watering practices and growing conditions. Clay is porous and allows more rapid drying, while plastic holds water for a longer period.

**12** Fill the pot about half to two thirds full with styrofoam peanuts. Place the oldest pseudobulb against the rim of the pot.

**13** Add potting medium to within one half-inch inch (1.25 cms) of the top of the pot. Do not cover the rhizome and make sure it is level with the top of the medium. The plant's climbing habit makes it appear to be leaning forward. Don't worry, as this will allow the emerging roots to immediately enter the fresh medium.

**14** Once the pot is filled with medium, place a rhizome clip between the pseudobulbs and over the rhizome. Press it down over the edge of the pot. If using a plastic pot, you may need to tighten the clip or use one designed for plastic pots. Tall plants may need a straight stake or ring stake to stabilize them. Be sure the orchid is firmly seated and does not wobble.

**15** Here is how the finished orchid should look. Don't forget the name tag! Some growers withhold water for a week or two to encourage roots to seek moisture. We prefer to water newly potted plants normally but keep them slightly shadier for a few weeks. The only roots remaining are healthy and the medium is fresh, so there is no root or medium degradation.

# REPOTTING A TYPICAL HOME-CENTER DENDROBIUM

*Evergreen dendrobiums have short rhizomes, and fine roots, and are happiest in slightly-too-small plastic pots. So when they are repotted it is important that they are staked and stable.*

1 As always, begin your potting session by sterilizing your cutting tools. Remember to resterilize between plants. A butane torch for flaming the tools is the most reliable way of disinfecting your tools.

2 This hybrid is a *Dendrobium phalaenopsis* type. Such plants are often overpotted in a fine peat-based mix. Usually, you will find that the old root ball from the smaller pot in which it was originally grown is still intact. If the plant has finished flowering and is showing new growth, it is a good idea to get it into a fresh medium.

3 Squeeze the plastic pot all around to loosen the plant from the pot. If the dendrobium is in a clay pot, use a knife or lever to free the roots. This is seldom necessary with plants purchased from garden centers.

4 Although the roots are not in very good condition, there are enough good, live roots that this orchid should begin growth quickly. Remove the old potting medium with your fingers.

5 Cut off the old bloom spike and carefully begin trimming away old dead roots. If there are any old, shriveled pseudobulbs that appear to be seedling growth, you may remove them for a better fit in the new pot.

6 Because evergreen dendrobium have short rhizomes and fine roots they can be potted in smaller pots than say, a cattleya. They also appreciate ample moisture when they are in growth, so we will use a plastic pot. Select one that will allow for about two-years growth. However, err on the side of a pot that appears too small rather than one that might seem a little large. Dendrobiums, in general, prefer to be under-potted, where they can be frequently watered and dry between waterings. They also seem to be generally intolerant of too wet conditions that can occur if overpotted.

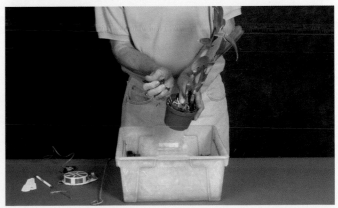

7 For this dendrobium we will use a bagged orchid mix that contains fir bark, charcoal, Aliflor, and perlite.

8 Add medium to within one-half inch (1.25 cms) of the pot rim, do not bury the base of the pseudobulbs. Tapping the plant gently on the potting surface during the potting process will aid in firming the plant in the pot.

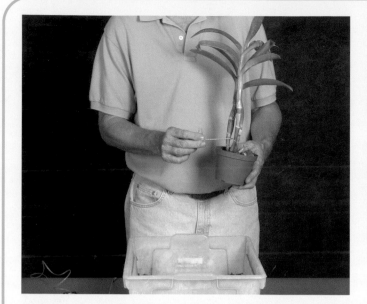

**9** Use a rhizome clip to secure the plant. You may need to tighten a standard clip to fit a plastic pot. Because you will be using a proportionately small pot, it is especially important that the plant be staked upright, because a plant that wobbles or is not straight in the pot will tend to fall over, making a mess and preventing the roots from establishing.

**10** Because of the height of this dendrobium plant we will use a straight stake to further stabilize the plant.

**11** Slip the stake over the edge of the pot, and use twist tie or wire to fasten the plant to the stake.

**12** Prepare a name tag with the name of the dendrobium. You can also add the date as it will help you decide when to repot the next time.

These types of "Dendrobium-phals" have long been a garden center favorite and will easily rebloom if given the proper conditions.

# REPOTTING A TYPICAL ONCIDIUM

*Orchids in the* Oncidium *alliance are vigorous producers of new roots.*
*So when growers are replacing the medium around their orchid, or moving up to a*
*larger size of pot, one of the major jobs is a careful pruning of the old roots.*

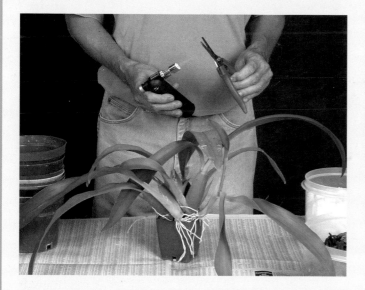

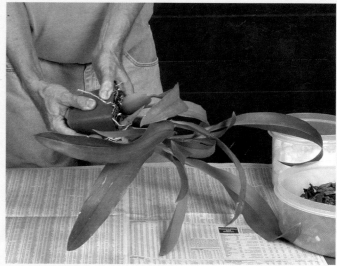

1 As always, begin your potting session by sterilizing your cutting tools. Remember to sterilize before each plant. If you keep a butane torch handy, this job is easy to remember. Torches with self-ignition are common and a great investment. This oncidium is growing over the edge of the pot, with fresh roots showing, and is ready to be repotted.

2 Squeeze the plastic pot all around to loosen the plant. It should easily lift out. If not, use a lever to gently pry the plant out of the pot. Because oncidiums are such rampant producers of roots, and because clay pots cannot easily be sterilized for reuse, you may find it easier on you and the plant to simply break the pot.

3 Although this plant is overgrown, the roots are in pretty good condition and there is a nice new growth. The root health is apparent by the clean white color and firm substance. Dead roots are dark or black and soft.

4 Loosen the root mass and remove the old potting medium with your fingers. The medium most commonly used for oncidiums is finer than for cattleyas and will often be fine and dust-like when broken down.

**5** If there are any old pseudobulbs at the back of the plant that are leafless or severely shriveled, you can remove them for a better fit in the new pot. Dress the cut with fungicide. Remove any old bloom spikes.

**6** Cut away any old, dead roots, which will be soft and generally brown or black. Trim the remaining roots to about 2/3 the depth of the pot into which the plant will be potted.

**7** Select a pot that will allow for about two-years growth. Choose plastic or clay, based upon your growing conditions and watering habits. Clay pots are porous and dry more quickly, while plastic pots are more water retentive. We will use fir bark mix for this oncidium.

**8** Place some drainage material in the bottom of the pot. This is especially important for growers who tend to water more often or in areas where the plant may be subject to summer rain.

**9** Press the medium down to firm it against the orchid roots. It is important that the plant be firm in the pot, because any wobbling or rocking may damage emerging root tips, resulting in the loss of the roots from the new growth.

**10** Here is the freshly repotted Oncidium hybrid, ready for a new year of growth. Don't forget the nametag!

# REPOTTING A TYPICAL
# VANDACEOUS ORCHID

*Vandaceous orchids can get straggly as they grow upward. Repotting
them requires a firm central stake that will help reposition
the plant's root mass closer to the center of gravity.*

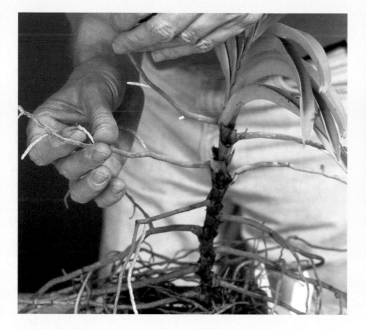

1 Begin by cutting off any old flower spikes. Here we see active new roots. Cut the stem just below the new roots.

2 Remove the old section that has mostly dead roots. Dead roots on vandaceous orchids usually appear dry and shriveled.

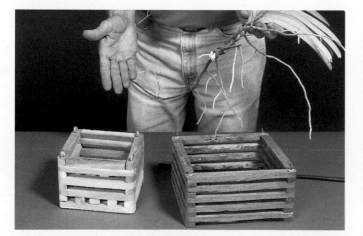

3 The basket on the right is larger than necessary whereas the basket on the left should provide an adequate home for several years, perhaps even until it begins to decay.

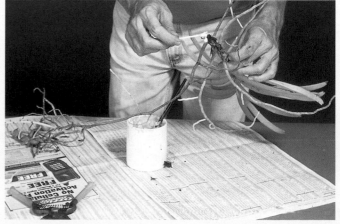

4 Don't forget to dab the cut stem with a little powdered fungicide mixed with water. Use a disposable cotton swab. This will protect the plant from infection.

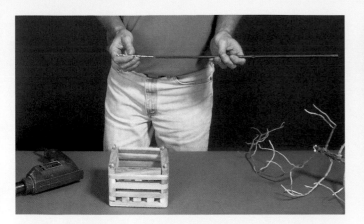

**5** You will need a bamboo stake to secure the vanda in the basket. Select a drill bit that is the same size or slightly smaller than the stake you intend to use. The stake must be firmly seated in the hole.

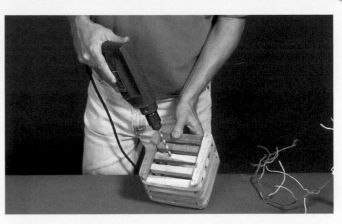

**6** Turn the basket over and locate the approximate center. If you need to, draw a line between opposing corners to find the center. Drill a hole. Drill slowly and carefully to avoid ramming the slat with the drill.

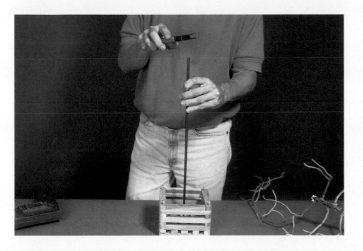

**7** Turn the basket right side up and work the stake into the hole. If necessary hammer it in.

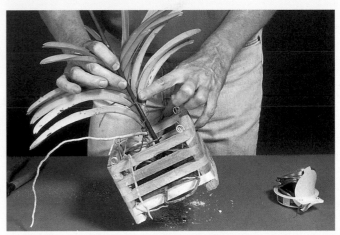

**8** Holding the plant so that the stem is up against the stake, use a tie material to securely fasten it.

**9** Use lineman's pliers to trim the stake to the height of the plant.

**10** Attach a wire hanger and name tag. Most vandaceous orchids are fine in an empty basket providing that you adjust your watering schedule to water them more frequently. If you wish, you may add a potting medium of your choice. Any coarse medium such as tree fern chunks, large lava rock, or large pieces of charcoal may be added to the basket.

# REPOTTING A TYPICAL PAPHIOPEDILUM

*Of all the orchids that need repotting, paphiopedilums are perhaps closest to a standard house plant in their requirements. Their lack of thick rhizomes make them one of the easiest orchids to repot.*

1 Paphiopedilums are usually easy to remove from their pots because their roots don't adhere tightly to surfaces. If necessary, use a tool for leverage.

2 If you plan to divide the plant, examine it to determine the logical separation point. Allow at least one mature growth and one new lead for each division.

3 The stolon between growths is soft and easily broken. Grab a division in each hand and snap the stolon so that you have two plants. If you prefer, you may use sterile shears.

4 This new growth should develop into the next flower-producing growth.

5 Mix a little fungicide with water into a smooth paste and dab on the cut stolon to prevent infection.

6 Begin cutting away any dead roots. With paphiopedilums, sometimes dead roots look no different to live roots. Generally, dead roots will originate from the old growth rather than the new lead.

7 Most growers prefer plastic pots for paphiopedilums, but clay could be used if you adjust your culture. Select the smallest pot possible that the stiff roots will fit comfortably into and allow for two-years growth. This is a good time to inspect the plant for any pests or other problems.

8 The best choice of medium to use depends on your growing conditions. We are using crumbled rockwool, coarse perlite, and a little fine fir bark. Add medium all around the plant to within one-half inch (1.25 cms) of the rim. Do not cover the base of the leaves.

9 A sharp tap on a firm surface will help settle the plant in the new medium.

10 Add a name tag and you are done! Because of a lack of thick rhizomes and the usually fine-textured potting medium used, paphiopedilums are among the easiest orchids to repot.

# REPOTTING A TYPICAL PHALAENOPSIS

*Some growers like to repot their phalaenopsis plants every year, so for lovers of the highly popular moth orchid this potting method should become a very familiar routine.*

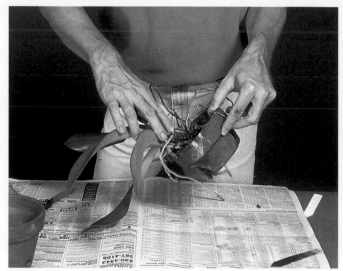

1 We will repot this phalaenopsis in a plastic pot and a fir bark medium. Fir bark may initially be difficult to wet, so presoaking in warm water will help condition it. If you wish, you may add a few drops of liquid detergent as a wetting agent.

2 Remove the phalaenopsis from its pot using your fingers or and oyster knife or dull chisel. Remove as much old medium from the roots as possible.

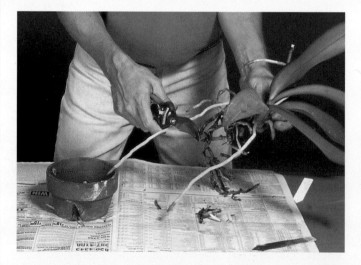

3 If there are any roots that are dry and shriveled or soft and mushy, use sterilized shears to cut them off.

4 Select a pot size that will accommodate the roots comfortably; roughly 1/3 to 1/2 of the total leaf span is a good rule of thumb.

5 Because plastic pots are lightweight and phalaenopsis tend to have tall flower spikes, we will use some river rock landscape stones as drainage material to keep the flowering plant from being top-heavy.

6 Center the orchid in the pot with the base of the leaves about one-half inch (1.25 cms) below the rim of the pot. Begin adding the dampened fir bark. Allow the leaves to sit above the medium.

7 Add the moistened fir bark until it is up to the base of the leaves. Do not bury the leaves.

8 Even though the medium may seem to hold the plant firmly, you should use a pot clip. Either a standard rhizome clip or a special clip for plastic pots will serve to anchor the plant by pressing the medium against the root mass.

9 Add the plant's name tag and you're done. Many growers of phalaenopsis like to repot them every year. Luckily, they are not difficult to pot.

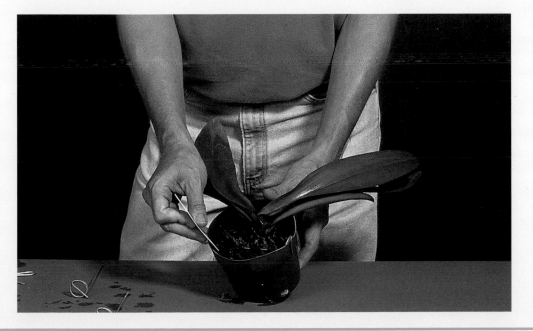

# ORCHID PESTS AND DISEASES

*Though less susceptible to disease than many plants, orchids still fall victim to pests and fungi that the grower can inadvertently introduce.*

Orchids are remarkable and resilient plants that tend to be unattractive to pests and resistant to disease. Orchids have evolved in high-stress environments and so are capable of enduring a considerable amount of environmental stress. However, if a plant is weakened by poor growing conditions, opportunistic pests may find a way to invade.

During orchid inspections, problems, such as infestation by an insect, a mite, or a disease may be found. Closer inspections with a 10x magnifying glass will show small insects and mites. Be sure to check the roots of ailing orchids, too.

The recommended treatments for insects, mites, fungi, and bacteria are not fixed and change with new laws and improved methods developed by chemical companies. Check with a professional resource to make sure a particular chemical is approved for orchids. Quizzing experts—among whom may be your county extension service or an experienced local nurseryman—is essential to learning. Local orchid societies often run orchid health-care clinics, while others may offer programs during the year on orchid ailments and their treatment.

Many acceptable products are not specifically labeled as suitable for orchids. Products labeled for general greenhouse use or with other nonspecific labeling may still be appropriate for orchids. However, you will have to rely on the advice of an orchid expert—anecdotal advice—as to what works, what doesn't, and what is not acceptable for certain classes of orchids.

Because most of the readers of this book will be beginners and will be growing their orchids in areas that may not always be appropriate for the application of harmful agricultural chemicals, we will focus on more benign methods. It is generally not a good idea to apply pesticides in a prophylactic manner. Use pesticides of any kind only to control infestations, not to prevent infestations. Otherwise, you will simply be assisting to produce resistant strains of pests.

Always follow the label directions when applying any pesticide. Keep the ingredients well mixed during application by shaking the sprayer periodically. Cover all plant surfaces completely for maximum effectiveness. Some people like to add a gentle horticultural soap to their mixture to give added efficacy.

Natural and synthetic horticultural oils are an effective method of pest control and are generally harmless to humans, animals, and plants. Those most often used are mineral oil and superfine oils, which are paraffin- or petroleum-based, highly refined oils. When sprayed onto orchids, these oils suffocate insect and mite pests by smothering their breathing pores. They work against aphids, mealybugs, spider mites, scale, thrips, and whiteflies. They are also effective against certain fungi and mildews.

Insecticidal soaps are widely available from garden centers and nursery suppliers as premixed spray solutions. Soaps kill insects and mites by removing or breaking down their protective coating. Insecticidal soaps are useful against soft-bodied insects, and mites such as aphids, mealybugs, scale crawlers, spider mites, thrips, and whiteflies. Complete coverage is essential for soaps to be effective and the spray must make good contact with the target pests. The soaps have no residual properties; so repeated applications at weekly intervals are indicated to reduce or eliminate pest populations.

Use caution when treating your orchids. Orchid flowers are especially sensitive. Foliar burn may result from repeat

Left: A mealybug in situ with the tell-tale brown discoloration.

Above: The damage inflicted after an attack of brown scale insects.

applications or blooms may be damaged, especially when the pesticide is mixed with hard water. To prevent injury, orchids should be shaded until the spray residues dry. Soaps are generally regarded as being rather benign for use around humans, animals, and plants. However, they may stimulate allergies and respiratory problems. Any pesticide should be always applied with care.

Growers easily control light infestations of mealybugs, aphids, or scale by using a cotton swab dipped in 70 percent isopropyl rubbing alcohol to wet or remove the insects. This method dissolves the insect's waxy covering. Using the swab enables you to reach pests hidden deep within sheaths and leaf crevices.

Some growers prefer to spray rubbing alcohol or a 50-50 mixture of water and alcohol with a misting bottle or small pump sprayer. Mix in a few drops of gentle, plant-safe liquid soap to the alcohol solution for maximum effectiveness. You can combine alcohol with insecticidal soaps but not with oils.

Other forward-thinking growers may use predatory insects such as green lacewings and ladybugs, which are beneficial insects for use in enclosed growing spaces like greenhouses. The larvae of green lacewings are voracious predators, consuming the eggs and immature stages of soft-bodied insects that attack orchids, including aphids, mealybugs, scale, spider mites, thrips, and whiteflies. Ladybug adults and larvae favor aphids and can consume more than 5,000 aphids each. They also eat other pests, including mites and scale. In addition, they consume insect eggs.

### Insects, Mites, Snails and Slugs

The best way to steer clear of insect infestation is to avoid introducing the pests with new plants. Always inspect new plants carefully to ensure that they are clean. Also, a clean growing area is the first line of defense against insect pests and disease, as both may build undetected populations in a sloppily kept growing area.

**Mealybugs** are oval to elliptical, cottony-appearing insects with threadlike protrusions around the horizontally ridged body. Mealybugs quickly form colonies on leaf and petal undersides, in crevices between leaves, and inside bud sheaths, causing stunted growth and yellowing leaves.

Physically remove mealybugs using a cotton swab dipped in 70 percent denatured or rubbing alcohol. Repeat every five to seven days until control is obtained. Weekly sprays with insecticidal soap, Orthene, Malathion, or horticultural oil are also effective.

**Aphids** are small, soft-bodied, usually green insects that cluster on areas of most rapid growth, such as new growth or flower stems. Honeydew, a sticky fluid secreted by the insects, attracts ants and provides a growth medium for sooty mold fungi. Treat as for mealybug. Spray with insecticidal soap, Orthene, Malathion, or horticultural oil. For minor infestations, remove insects by washing plants with warm water and mild detergent. (Note: many detergents may be toxic to orchids; however, mild soaps are often effective.)

**Scale insects** appear as hard-shelled, round, immobile, brown helmet-shaped objects that most often occur on the undersides of leaves and stems. Orchids are susceptible to several types of scale, including brown scale, soft scale, and Boisduval scale. Severe infestations can cause leaf yellowing and stunt the plant.

Like aphids, soft scale insects secrete honeydew, which attracts sooty mold fungi and ants. Treat light infestations by removing the scale with a swab dipped in 70 percent denatured or rubbing alcohol. Always inspect your plants regularly, removing insects as you find them. Control severe infestations by spraying with insecticidal soap, Orthene, Malathion, or horticultural oil.

Spraying is most effective on the tiny young scales or crawlers, which have no hard covering. Spray plants weekly for several weeks to kill crawlers at emergence from eggs. Boisduval scale, most often a problem on cattleyas, is a severe and very contagious pest that may be very difficult, if not impossible, to eradicate with available pesticides. The grower should carefully consider whether it is better to simply dump a badly infested plant rather than run the risk of having it infect the rest of the collection.

**Spider mites** appear as barely visible green or red specks on lower leaf surfaces. A 10x magnifying glass is helpful in

Below: Undisturbed soft scale insects can reproduce rapidly.

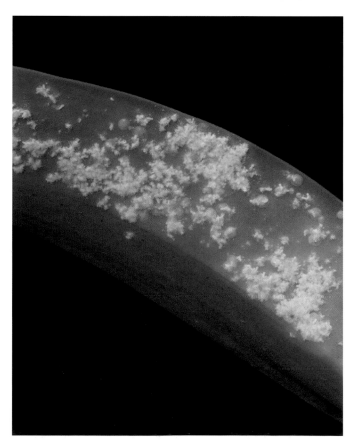

Below: Spider mite infestation.

**Right:** Cattleyas and vandas are particularly loved by thrips, which can damage the flowers you have waited all year to see.

**Below:** Black rot is one of the most destructive diseases of orchids, especially cattleyas. It can be spread by splashing water and will quickly destroy large numbers of plants, especially if they are grown close together.

seeing them. Leaves appear dusty with a silvery appearance, especially on the bottom where the mites are most active. Mites thrive in hot, dry, dusty conditions, so keep leaves clean. Also, when you are watering or misting, syringe under the leaves, because this helps to keep spider mite populations down. Another method of preventing mite attacks is to occasionally wash plants with warm water and mild detergent, remembering that many detergents may be toxic to orchids. For infested plants, spray leaves, especially the undersides, with insecticidal soap. Treat plants weekly for several weeks to kill mites as they emerge from eggs.

**Thrips** are very small, yellow or brown to black, winged insects that are a big problem, especially in warmer temperatures. Thrips most often come into the greenhouse or growing area as the weather warms, particularly as outside flowers begin to fade, forcing them to search out new feeding areas. Thrips suck the sap from orchid plants, dendrobiums and vandas are preferred hosts. Thrips damage to leaves, stems, and especially flowers may be severe and appears as brown or chlorotic spots, streaks,

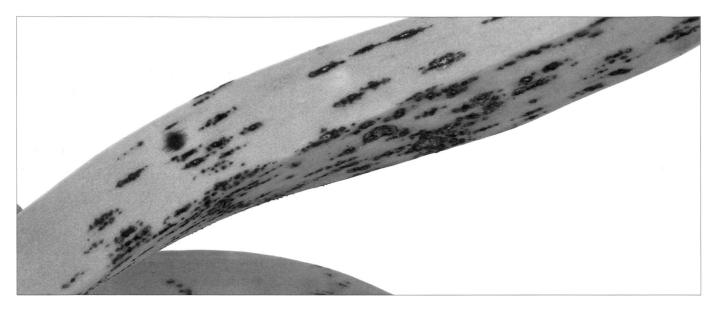

## Orchid Diseases

Orchids are generally disease resistant. However, when they are crowded so that air cannot freely circulate, problems are more likely—as well as more difficult to detect before they become severe. Sanitary growing conditions are the number one preventative to avoiding diseases on orchids indoors. As with insecticides, few fungicides are available to the home orchid grower and even fewer fungicides can be used indoors.

When selecting a fungicide, read the label carefully to ensure that it is labeled for indoor use on orchids and that it controls the disease(s) in question.

In complete contradiction to the course of action advised for dealing with pests, the old adage "an ounce of prevention is worth a pound of cure" is completely true for diseases. It is especially important in its application as so few commercially available preparations are effective. Far better is the removal of the diseased area, allowing clean, dry air to reach it. Oxygen is nature's cure-all for disease. If a plant is severely infected, it may be more cost-effective to simply discard it because it will be so difficult to completely cure and it will continue to serve as source of infection for your other plants. Some plants just seem to be more susceptible, and the grower has to ask if the plant is worth the trouble or if another might better take its place.

Cattleyas and phalaenopsis are especially susceptible to

and discoloration of plant tissues. For indoor growing areas, including windowsills, try insecticidal soap for controlling thrips. Outdoor or greenhouse hobbyists may prefer Malathion or Orthene, applied weekly. Pesticides do not easily control thrips. Because they are so mobile, they simply leave during spraying and return afterwards.

**Slugs and snails** are betrayed by the trail of slime they leave behind. Affected plants have chewed leaf and petal margins and holes in buds. Slime trails lace across flowers, leaves, and other surfaces. Use slug bait for large outbreaks, but keep bait away from pets. Diatomaceous earth or iron phosphate (Sluggo) may be placed around the base of orchids to prevent slug and snail attacks.

black-rot fungus, as is any orchid left standing in water or in decomposing growing medium. Soft, rotted areas begin on leaves or new growth and then spread into rhizomes. Infected leaves are initially purplish brown then turn black. Remove infected areas, cutting into healthy tissue. Sterilize cutting tools after each cut. Isolate the plant in a low-humidity area to dry off. Water carefully until the plant recovers. Repot with fresh growing medium.

This treatment is also appropriate for other fungal diseases such as root-rot fungus, bacterial brown spot, and leaf-spot fungus. Botrytis, or petal blight, is best controlled by keeping your growing area free of dead flowers, which serve as a source of infection. Botrytis is also symptomatic of overly high nighttime humidity, so another preventative measure is to vent your greenhouse thoroughly during the afternoon to allow humidity to fall slightly in compensation for lowering temperatures and the rising relative humidity at night.

Orchids are subject to viruses, much the same as almost all other plants. Diagnosis is complicated by symptoms that resemble problems such as nutrient disorders. Viruses are incurable; destroy infected plants. Plants may carry viruses without symptoms, so sterilize cutting tools between uses. Space plants to keep them from touching. Some private and university-based laboratories will test to determine if an orchid is infected with a virus. However, since viruses in orchids are incurable, it is best to discard infected orchids and start over with virus-free plants.

**Below:** As devastating as disease, cold can damage orchids.

**Below:** A virused plant.

# BUYING AND SHOWING ORCHIDS

*All that glistens is not necessarily gold with a few showy garden center orchids. There are some basic rules about choosing which particular plant to buy that should never go unheeded.*

The excitement and beauty of an exotic, flowering orchid plant has lured many buyers into ill-considered decisions. While most flowering plants commonly seen in mass-market arenas are proven as flowering potted plants, i.e. the flowers are showy and long-lasting, there may be the odd one or two that are not. Also, for most people obtaining plants at mass-market outlets, the sheer longevity of the floral display makes the purchase cost effective, whether or not the plant survives to flower again.

However, for those gardeners who enjoy growing their plants and who are looking for something a little different, there is a multitude of choice available that goes far beyond the offerings of even the local garden center. Dedicated orchid vendors will want you to succeed with their plants, but they will assume that you possess a certain level of expertise unless you tell them specifically otherwise. Don't be afraid to tell the seller that you are not widely experienced and that you can use all the help you can get.

When contemplating the purchase of an orchid there are a few basic things to look out for and avoid.

- If the plant—not the flowers, the plant itself—looks poorly
- If the leaves are wilted or otherwise damaged
- If the plant is not secure in the pot, thereby demonstrating poor roots
- If the flowers are all wide open

In other words, the plant should be fresh, well-rooted, and with buds yet to open to be a good purchase option. If the flowers are just so distinctive and desirable that you must have *that* particular plant, and the plant is simply poorly grown or run down, it is okay to go ahead and purchase it,

with the advance knowledge that you will have to nurse it back to health. If your conditions do not permit good, healthy plant growth and your existing plants just about survive, not thrive, you may want to think twice about a plant that is already doing poorly.

Just because an orchid is sold in your local garden center doesn't necessarily mean that it will be easy to grow in home conditions. Most homes are lacking good-quality light and have fairly low humidity. To overcome these two limiting factors, home orchids have to be suitable for lower light conditions and tolerant of lower humidity.

The most widely sold orchid, the moth orchid, or phalaenopsis, meets these criteria admirably. Not only that, they also grow to flowering size very quickly under industrial greenhouse conditions, enabling commercial growers to churn out a good quality product that can be sold for a reasonable price.

Almost all of the flowering orchid plants in the mass market meet this commercial criterion: they have to be able to be produced quickly, reliably, and at a reasonable cost. Another orchid that meets the ideal of flowering under lower light conditions and tolerating low humidity is the slipper orchid or paphiopedilum. However, the often bizarre flowers are definitely an acquired taste and, despite modern breeding and technological innovations, the plants are slower growing and less reliable in quality than many other orchids. Nevertheless, slippers are worth searching out if only because of their exceptionally long flower life, potentially measured in months rather than weeks.

Until fairly recently, the next most commonly seen garden center orchid was the phalaenopsis-type dendrobium, nicknamed Den phal. This is unfortunate for so many reasons.

While the flowers are showy and long lasting, superficially resembling those of phalaenopsis, and the plants are generally available at very reasonable prices, they require high light, heat, and good humidity to have any chance of reblooming. In other words, they are highly unsatisfactory for continued home growing. Their popularity has been based on their rapid growth to flowering under tropical conditions and a good shelf life.

For growers in areas where out-of-door culture is possible during some or all of the year, the Den phals make wonderful patio plants with multiple flowerings per year of several to many sprays of colorful blooms. However, for the home, the plants are simply too big and too unlikely to flower again to be worthwhile as anything other than a disposable potted plant.

Today, intergeneric oncidium types are rapidly overtaking the Den phals' place alongside phalaenopsis. These are highly colorful and long lasting, with the advantage of an almost limitless color palette, as well as being much more likely to allow success to the home gardener. The plants are generally of moderate size, to about 20 inches (50 cms), with often-branching sprays that may be more than 40 inches (100 cms) long. While requiring more light than phals, this type is much more likely to rebloom under typical home conditions, and, if the grower has any patio space at all to give to summer growing, good results are almost assured.

Once these three or four basic types are exhausted, though, the budding orchid fanatic will have to take a bit more time in finding appropriate sources of the type of plants that are both to their liking and relatively easy to grow under the conditions they can provide. Additionally, the aspiring orchid grower will often find it relatively easy to adapt their existing home conditions—whether indoors by a bay window with a favorable east, south, or west exposure; a sunroom; or a patio—to a wide array of fairly easily available orchids.

## Orchids by Internet

Until the last ten years or so, those wishing to grow a wide array of orchid types had two main sources: a drive to the nearest orchid dealer, or mail order catalogs. Several factors have conspired to radically change this. First, the ever-escalating price of gas has considerably shortened the reasonable driving range. Next, truly local orchid growers have been finding it more and more difficult to make ends meet and have been closing.

The Internet has made the traditional orchid catalog almost obsolete. This, in a way, represents the loss of a wonderful resource, because the old school orchid catalog was the source of a lot of valuable information that may not always be posted to a grower's Internet site.

**Below:** Producing show quality orchids such as this *Paphiopedilum* St. Swithin 'Crystelle' FCC/AOS takes much dedication. This plant was the Grand Champion at the 2005 Miami International Orchid Show and impressed the judges enough to award it an AOS First Class Certificate.

On the other hand, with sensible shopping, the Web has opened up a vast array of orchid sources to the general public. However, some of the same good, common-sense rules apply to the purchase of plants from an Internet supplier as from a catalog vendor. The first rule is that just because someone produces a good web site or catalog, it doesn't make him or her a good orchid grower.

The savvy orchid buyer does research first. Have any friends or fellow orchid society members bought from this source? Are there any ratings posted on the various web-based services? Are the prices reasonable for the presumptive plant size? This is a good thing to look into, because the pot size seldom, if ever, is a good indication of plant size. Some growers like to grow the plant as large as possible in a given pot size and allow the new grower to shift up into the next size pot. Other growers find it preferable to offer their plants in pots that allow another year's growth before potting is required. Still others pot the plant on into a larger pot and offer the plant when it is still quite small for the size of the pot.

This is also a critical bit of information for another important reason. Some home growers' conditions do not allow them to succeed well with very small or young plants or those that have been recently repotted. Also, a plant that has only recently been repotted and is not well established, ships poorly and is stressed in transit, so making acclimatization to new conditions more difficult. Two good

---

**Below:** Spectacular orchid displays like this are a feature of the major orchid shows around the country.

general sources of orchid information and centralized vendor information are the American Orchid Society Web site (www.orchidweb.org/aos) and the Orchid Mall (www.orchidmall.com), an independently-run Web site.

Both of the sites provide good general information; the American Orchid Society's Web site is a source of traditionally "vetted" info, while the Orchid Mall's information comes from such a broad cross section that discerning growers are expected to draw their own conclusions.

## Orchid Fairs

One of the most profound revolutions in the orchid business of the past few years has been the establishment of orchid shows and fairs as significant players in the orchid-vending arena. In years past, a visit to your local orchid grower was the best way to browse and select from an array of orchid plants. Orchid shows were seasonal and the vendors' selection was not always wide ranging.

Today orchid shows, particularly those with any national or international pretensions, will have a broad array of orchid growers from around the U.S., Hawaii, and occasionally, Latin America or Asia. Indeed, a new breed of orchid shows, popularly known as orchid fairs, have sprung up. There, a group of vendors get together with the specific intent of drawing people to see their wares.

These events resemble orchid shows but without the official orchid displays, though the individual growers often put on such good-looking sales booths, stocked with flowering and sample plants, that the uninitiated would have a hard time differentiating from a traditional orchid show. Don't be overwhelmed and overlook the need for the same sort of due diligence that you would exercise when researching a vendor on the Internet.

Too often, you will find that the vendors haven't actually grown the plants they are selling, and this can be a warning sign unless the salespeople on duty show evidence of knowing something about their plants. If they are knowledgeable and helpful, look a little further. If they are not, walk away.

One of the best aspects of buying directly from vendors who are also growers is that—because they are only able to display a small portion of their wares—they make sure to bring only the very best they have of any given item. This, in effect, preselects for you. There will often be example plants in bloom, whether siblings of unbloomed seedlings to show an orchid's potential, or flowering plants of meristems, where you'll know exactly what you will be purchasing.

## Orchid Societies

Once you've begun to branch out a bit in your orchid hobby, growing plants on a year or two after purchase and flowering them yourself, you may feel confident enough to display them to show off your plant husbandry skills. Of course, you may have already joined a local orchid society, one of the very best places for gaining the sort of local knowledge you will need to grow your plants well. Members of local societies are, for the most part, generous with their knowledge and often with propagations from their own plants.

The American Orchid Society Web site, noted previously, has a comprehensive listing of AOS-affiliated societies. Most local societies have a monthly meeting at which members can display their flowering plants. There is often ribbon judging where the plants are judged against what is on display at the meeting and a chance to see what others in your area find successful for them.

Once you are comfortable in your local society, you many find that you want to participate in a national society, such as the American Orchid Society. Membership in a national group not only provides a periodic journal, such as the *AOS Orchids Magazine*, but also helps to support the many orchid-oriented programs of national hobbyist groups.

The AOS also has a world-renowned judging system with regional judgings and show judgings around the country and throughout the year, with over 200 opportunities to have your plant evaluated by diligently trained judges.

AOS judging is quality judging, as opposed to ribbon or show, judging. Quality judging evaluates the flowers on their quality in comparison to others of their type and breeding, usually on an international scale of knowledge. One way to understand the difference between ribbon/show judging and quality judging is to remember that it is the difference between the best German shepherd here today and a good German shepherd based on knowledge of what the breed ought to be. Wherever you choose to display your plant, it should be well grown and displayed, with dead leaves removed and inflorescences properly staked.

# FOUR SEASONS OF ORCHIDS

*With an almost worldwide distribution that includes every conceivable ecological niche, orchids stand supreme in the plant kingdom for their beauty and diversity.*

So much relating to the passage of time is an artificial construct imposed by man. Seconds, minutes, hours, weeks, and months are all examples of man's need to organize and understand. Seasons, though, are a bit more problematic if one is not attuned to nature's cyclical pace because any season's length is so dependent on the observer's distance from the equator and elevation above sea level. Nevertheless, no matter how long or short each particular season may be in your location, everyone has experience of their own winter, spring, summer, and fall.

The reactions of living beings to seasonal changes are the result of a complex interplay involving day length, the sun's angle above the horizon, temperature, and other factors. Exactly how and why any organism perceives that it is spring or fall is peculiar to that being. Generally, the inhabitants of any latitude and elevation come to agree through their various methods on when one season arrives or departs for the next. Nor is the definition between seasons a hard and fast line in the sands of time. The division between seasons is barely perceptible. However, we can all recall a day in late winter when we just knew that spring was on its way—and soon it was.

Orchids respond to seasonal changes in much the same way as other plants do. Their seasonal reactions are vital to ensuring that their growth cycle matches nutrient and water availability in their habitat and that their flowering period coincides with the pollinator's presence. One of the most important reasons we can have orchids flowering throughout all seasons is their extraordinarily wide distribution. In other words, no matter the month, somewhere there is an orchid seeking pollination. In describing the season of any particular orchid's bloom, man again seeks to impose his order.

Traditionally, orchid seasons are a little different than the calendar may tell us. For convenience, we will use the seasonal breakdowns that you are most likely to find in the various outlets where you acquire your plants. Also, while we are going to use months to delineate these seasons, it is wise to remember that seasons blend one into the next. A late-winter bloomer in one place may be considered an early-spring bloomer elsewhere. We will attempt to note these aberrations as we discuss the various plants. The seasons we will be using are:

- **Winter** – December, January, February
- **Spring** – March, April, May
- **Summer** – June, July, August
- **Fall** – September, October, November

For each season we will include a boxed summary, showing what to expect in the way of conditions and how to treat your plants for their best performance. Each season will begin with a general overview, with each of the major types getting their own boxed summary that outlines the preferred treatment during that season.

As a final caveat, the season of any given orchid is an approximation. A plant may be spring blooming, purchased in flower in March, yet rebloom earlier or later by several weeks depending on the care given and the particular location in which it is grown. Thankfully, orchid flowers are so long lasting that the overlap between plants will take care of any shortfall. You can always find room for one more plant!

# WINTER-FLOWERING ORCHIDS

*When the winter sun dips low in the sky, the moth and slipper orchids, which thrive in marginal light conditions, come to the fore.*

## WINTER CARE

### GENERAL

**Day length:** Shortest of the year; increasing toward the end of season; plants begin to respond with growth and/or flower initiation.

**Light:** Weakest, with sun at lowest angle, often influenced by cloud cover. Conversely, may be exceptionally bright and potentially burning owing to atmosphere clearing after rain.

**Temperature:** Almost uniformly cool or cold, with exception of very southerly areas, such as south Florida; frost a persistent threat.

**Overall:** Plants rest or grow very slowly; metabolism is at slowest point when flowering.

### GROWER RESPONSE

**Watering:** Infrequent, every seven to ten days or fewer under gray conditions.

**Fertilizer:** Infrequent, every third watering at low concentration of one-quarter label strength or less; good time for low-nitrogen formulation.

**Watch for:** Potential burn from areas unshaded by deciduous trees or a suddenly clear atmosphere.

Winter is the most difficult season for most novice orchid growers. Plants that are naturally dormant, or nearly so, during the short and cool days do not need much in the way of grower attention. This is contrary to the popular misconception that orchids always require a lot of care. They do not. During the winter months, tropical orchids' growth is at a near standstill. Metabolic processes are at their slowest pace of the year. Very little water is being taken up by the root system, and with a drastically slowed or completely stopped growth rate, the need for any fertilizer is at the lowest point of the year. Indeed, if you were to completely stop all fertilizing during the three months of winter, your plants would be far better off than if you over-fertilized. Day and night temperatures should also be in balance. If day temperatures in your growing area are only reaching the high 60s Fahrenheit (18–21°Celsius), you can afford to run the night temperatures down into the 50s Fahrenheit (10–15°Celsius) with little fear, as long as you are observing your plants' watering needs and not keeping them too wet. Not only does this save on energy, it makes good sense. If temperatures in the growing area are forced artificially high, day and night, and you are frequently watering and fertilizing, plants will put on very weak, soft growth, because there is simply not the good-quality light necessary for strong growth. Not only will this soft growth be more susceptible to plant disease and pests, but the effort that goes into making it may not be compensated for by the metabolic products it can produce, resulting in a net loss and a weaker plant. So, keep your watering and fertilizing to a minimum during winter months, in concert with the lower temperatures and weaker light.

### Flowering Patterns

While many orchid plants are nearly dormant during winter months and show little vegetative growth, there is a good amount of activity on the flowering front. Orchids flower to attract pollinators and to do this, the flowers must be visible. Often, winter months in orchid habitats are when the forest canopy is at its least dense, making the orchid flowers more easily seen by potential pollinators.

And, no orchid says winter glory better than *Phalaenopsis*. While modern horticultural techniques have made it possible to have phals in bloom at almost any time of the year, winter is when they normally bloom and when they are naturally at their best. Winter flowering orchids, in general, develop their flowering stems slowly owing to the shorter days and lower temperatures. Their flowers also have the opportunity to open and develop slowly, resulting in larger blooms with harder substance and consequently better-lasting qualities. Because growers do not have to resort to any special techniques to ensure winter flowering in phals, the plants can be allowed to develop at their own pace, and give their best, longest-lasting floral display.

**Below:** *Dtps.* Sweet Strawberry. Plants that once would have only been available to the aficionado at an astronomical cost are seen week in and week out at retail outlets around the U.S.

# PHALAENOPSIS

## WINTER CARE FOR PHALAENOPSIS

**Light:** Allow all possible light to reach the plants to ensure development of inflorescences with maximum flower count.

**Temperature:** Maintain at no less than 60° Fahrenheit (16° Celsius) nights, and 75° Fahrenheit (24° Celsius) days.

**Water:** Developing inflorescence may necessitate more frequent watering than might otherwise be indicated.

**Fertilizer:** Low nitrogen to encourage maximum flower potential.

**Watch for:** Mealybugs love to hide out in the bracts at each node of the flower stem; scale may also be a problem on flowers and stems. Use alcohol and cotton swabs to clean up smaller infestations, soap and oil combination for larger ones.

There is no display more beautiful than an arching stem of white "moths," exemplified by *Phal. amabilis*, one of the progenitor species of our modern white phals. However, the plants we see today of this species are far

---

**Right:** *Phal. amabilis* are compact plants, often no more than 15" (38 cms) across. They produce one or two often branching inflorescences in midwinter. The flower stems are strong and upright and about one half the height of typical hybrid phals. They grow to 18" (46 cms), bearing eight to twelve or more 3" (8 cms) pristine white blooms. Care as for all phals.

---

**Below:** *Phal. equestris* is almost a dwarf phal species. Growing to 12" (30 cms) across at maturity, it is quite happy in a 4" (10 cms) pot. Upright, slightly arching sprays of pink blushed white blooms with red lips appear in midwinter. Blooms are petite, about 1" to 2" (2.5–5 cms), with bold red lips. Care as for all phals.

Doritaenopsis hybrids, *Dtps*. Newberry Parfait 'Picotee' AM/AOS (**right**) and *Dtps*. Chain Xen Pearl *Phal*. (**opposite**) are known as "standard" phalaenopsis. These plants represent the best of traditional phal breeding. They can grow to over 36" (91 cms) across in greenhouse situations but are more commonly 24–30" (61–76 cms) across in the home. Upright stems may grow to 36" (91 cms) or more and bear up to a dozen or so 4" (10 cms) flowers in a variety of colors. Keep evenly moist and regularly fed. A western exposure works best. Repotting is best done in late spring, when new roots begin to emerge from the base of the plant. Mature plants may go back into the same size pot, using new medium. Keep shady until established.

removed from their jungle origins, often the result of seven or more generations of nursery breeding. Another phalaenopsis species important in the breeding of the more modern miniature hybrids is *Phal. equestris*. Again, the plants seen today are many generations removed from their forest ancestors. Both *Phal. amabilis* and *Phal. equestris* benefit from generations of selection. They show increased flower quality and improved vigor and floriferousness. Such selection is often overlooked by hobbyists bent on getting the best flowers, but savvy professionals select for plant growth habits first because the ease with which a plant grows and flowers is key to their profitability.

Nor are phals simply white flowers any more. Over 100 years of breeding, capped by two decades of intense work by the Taiwanese, have resulted in a color palette in phals that is second to none. From the soft colors of the more traditional *Dtps*. Newberry Parfait to the exotic hues of *Dtps*. Chain Xen Pearl to the exceptionally dark *Dtps*. Brother Pungoteaque Creek, this group has seen extraordinary progress. Strong yellow phalaenopsis, once only the dream of a few visionary breeders, are now rather commonly available, even at retail outlets. Plants such as *Dtps*. Sogo Pearl and *Phal*. Margarita Lime, which would have once brought hundreds of dollars and been available only to the select few, are common sights on nursery benches. Improvement in traditional colors and types has not stood still. Pink, pink striped, and spotted phals are better than ever before. *Phal*. Mem. 'Cecilia Rimlin' exemplifies the high level of striped pinks today, while *Phal*. Paul Tatar x Sweet Revenge shows the high degree to which striped flowers have risen. Spotted phals, once dominated by *Phal. stuartiana*'s influence, are now more boldly marked than ever, with heavier substance and better-lasting quality, as seen in *Phal*. Brother Redland Spots. Indeed, the spotting on phals has become so thoroughly saturated that a new type, the Harlequin, with nearly coalesced spotting can be seen in *Dtps*. Ho's Exotic Twist. Finally, miniature phals, with their compact plant habit and multitudes of flowers, have also been highly developed, as in *Phal*. Little Mary. There are too many beautiful plants to name each and every one but all have their particular appeal and all are at their best during the winter months. Additionally, their long-lasting floral display—often for weeks to a month or more—provides one of the best flower values on the market today.

**Left:** *Phal.* Mem. 'Cecilia Rimlin'. Striped phals are perennial favorites for their bright and cheery appearance. This type will often bear two or more branching inflorescences in maturity, with a shower of medium size, 3" (8 cms) blooms that last for months. Flowers such as the one here are prized for their sharpness of markings over a brilliant rose background and striking red lip. Care as for other phals.

**Below:** *Dtps.* Pungoteague Creek 'Sun Bulb' HCC/AOS. These plants are of standard size, and grow to 18" (46 cms). Flowers may tend to be bunched toward the end of the inflorescence. Care as for other phals.

**Right:** *Dtps.* Sogo Pearl.

**Below:** *Phal.* Margarita Lime. Great strides have been made with yellow phalaenopsis in recent times. Yellows are richer and clearer, spotting is more distinct and shape is more rounded and closer to the standard size of 3–4" (8–10 cms). Flower stems may need staking for best upright display. Plants can lack floriferousness, giving only a few flowers per stem, though with branching a more flowers appear. Plants are roughly the same size as most readily available phals, but foliage tends to be brighter, green, and slightly softer, hence they are more susceptible to physical damage or disease. However, the flowers have such heavy substance that they may last even longer than other types.

**Left and right:** *Phal.* Brother Redland Spots (very spotted) and *Dtps.* Ho's Exotic Twist ('Harlequin') require standard phalaenopsis care. The modern red types may have slightly lower flower count, four or six 3" (8 cms) flowers per upright stem. Spotted types, depending on their breeding, may have fewer flowers, like the reds, or more, like the multiflora miniatures. All are in the medium-size range of 3" (8 cms). The Harlequins are the most recently developed and tend to have more floral anomalies than other types, although the flowers are good sized: 3" (8 cms) or so.

**Left:** *Phal.* Little Mary. *Phal. equestris* has sired an entire race of miniature multiflora phals such as *Phal.* Little Mary. Plants will grow up to 24" (61 cms) or more across at maturity and bear massive branching spikes up to 30" (76 cms). They have dozens of brightly striped 2" (5 cms) blooms. A mature plant may bear three or four flowering stems. Care as for all phals.

# CATTLEYAS

Cattleyas, in all their various forms, bloom throughout the year. However, with a little bit of background knowledge, one can almost know the season by the particular types and species that happen to be in bloom. Winter-blooming cattleyas are headed up by *C. jenmanii*, often blooming as early as late November. As with almost all of the unifoliate, or one leaved, cattleyas, *C. jenmanii* comes in several color forms besides the typical lavender form, such as coerulea, or blue. Known as the Christmas Cattleya, *C. percivaliana* is recognized by its more compact stature, sparkling lavender color, and richly yellow-marked lip. Because it is so compact for the type, it can easily be grown into a floriferous specimen plant in a relatively small pot. Sadly, some do not appreciate its rather musky scent. Latest winter blooming among the unifoliate cattleyas is the famous Colombian cattleya, *C. trianaei*. Long a favorite parent for cut-flower growers, *C. trianaei* is well-known for

**Left:** *C. percivaliana*. The 'Christmas Cattleya,' *C. percivaliana* is recognizable by its very compact stature, which makes it amenable to windowsills and home growing. Some object to its musky perfume, most powerful during the day. *C. percivaliana* comes in the same array of color types as other unifoliate cattleyas. *C. percivaliana* seems to be more tolerant of cool conditions than other cattleyas.

**Above:** *C. jenmanii* Coerulea. Typical of winter-blooming unifoliate cattleyas, *C. jenmanii* flowers from a lead that grows during summer months and briefly rests. Plants are 12–18" (30–46 cms) tall and bear two to four large flowers. Grow as for other cattleyas, withholding water to some extent as winter approaches.

imparting its exceptionally full form and broad petals to its progeny, even those many generations removed, as in the many progeny of *C.* Horace such as *Blc.* Nina de Primavera. Of course, there are always those hybrids, such as *Pot.* Mariah, where the *C. trianaei* influence is so far removed that only the season, affected by other species as well, remains. One of *C. trianaei*'s best features in a breeding sense is that it is not as dominant for lavender color as those hybrids derived from *C. labiata*, so allows more of the unusual yellow, orange, and red colors to come through.

While unifoliate, large-flowered cattleya species and

hybrids were the darlings of the traditional cut-flower grower. The smaller, brighter blooms of the Central American species, *C. aurantiaca*, set the stage for a new range of floriferous potted plants. The first hybrids in this group were made early in the development of modern cattleya hybrids but have begun to reach their potential more recently as growers search for compact varieties that provide a wealth of blooms from smaller and faster-growing plants. Starting with the old favorite, *Lc.* Gold Digger, and progressing through *Lc.* Magic Bell, this group has remained fairly close to its species influences, while maximizing their appeal.

There is an assortment of beautiful cattleya hybrids that bloom regularly and well in the winter season, such as *Ctyh.* Landwoods, *Lc.* Hsinying Excell and *Lc.* Hawaiian Easter, three distinctly beautiful color variations. *Blc.* Morning Song, derived from *B. nodosa* ancestry, is more typical of a type that blooms later in the year. Both *Epicyclia* Mabel Kanda and *Blc.* Suncoast Sunspots demonstrate the variety present in winter bloomers, as does *Pot.* Aztec's Red Beauty, a type more typical of fall blooming cattleyas. Finally, there is an assortment of fine species in the cattleya-alliance that are less traditionally attractive but still appealing, like *Epi. ciliare*. Matching the less traditional types in their appeal is the Mexican species, *L. anceps*, which closely resembles a small cattleya. An entire subgroup of cattleya hybrids utilizing *L. anceps* has sprung up owing to its cold tolerance. This type of cattleya hybrid makes excellent garden plants to accompany cymbidiums and similar garden subjects. *Lc.* Puppy Love is a perfect example of a fine *L. anceps* hybrid. Some experienced growers consider it one of the top cattleya hybrids ever produced, owing to its long-lasting blooms, multiple flowerings per year, and sheer beauty.

**Left:** With its delicate color and full shape, *C. trianaei* represents the archetypal large-flowered cattleya. Mature *C. trianaei* plants can grow to 20" (51 cms) tall or more. The plants are not always free branching, making them a one-flower stem per pot subject. Growers observe their plants and pot when new roots emerge from the base of the newest growth.

**Right:** *C. aurantiaca.* This Central American species is one of the nicest cattleyas for display purposes. Plants range from a compact 12" to more than 18" (30–46 cms) tall, depending on the particular cultivar. Most are free branching, giving a multitude of flowering stems per plant in the midwinter season. *C. aurantiaca* is more accepting of cooler temperatures than many.

**Left:** *Lc.* Gold Digger, 'Orglade's Mandarin'. This hybrid has proven to be an all-time favorite, owing to its floriferous nature. It easily gives multiple clusters of brilliant golden yellow blooms in late winter, perfect for the earliest shows. Commonly seen in the trade, several cultivars are available thanks to tissue culture. All make fine plants for the home, frost-free garden, or greenhouse. The best results are seen with plants that are allowed to grow into large specimens. Plants reach 18" (46 cms) or so and branch freely, easily giving a spectacular show in a 6–8" (15–20 cms) pot.

**Right:** *Lc.* Hsinying Excell. This 8" (20 cms) tall cattleya is an excellent choice for indoor growing. Plant in an undersize pot. Suits very bright light and can be allowed to dry between waterings. Its 2" (5 cms) flowers are very long lasting.

**Below:** *Lc.* Hawaiian Easter. This cattleya gets its compact habit from C. Angelwalker, bred from the dwarf C. *walkeriana*. Its large blooms are very long lasting. As with *Lc.* Hsinying Excell, grow in a rather small pot and allow to dry well between waterings.

**Left:** *Blc.* Morning Song. The Hawaiians have been very active in the production of novel new cattleyas, many based on breeding with *Brassavola nodosa*, the Lady of the Night. Even a generation removed from the species, hybrids with *B. nodosa* retain their species charm. They remain very easy to grow and fairly compact, here no more than 15" (38 cms) tall, with blooms that can reach 6" (15 cms) or more. Hawaiian breeders attend orchid shows throughout the U.S. each year, so availability of this type is very good.

**Left:** *Blc.* Suncoast Sunspots 'Tinkerbell' HCC/AOS. Spotted cattleya hybrids remain the domain of the specialist, but occasionally a clone will become highly popular. At their best, this type is strong growing and standard sized for a cattleya, around 18–24" (46–61 cms). The cluster of boldly marked blooms is very long lasting. 'Tinkerbell' is exceptional for the clarity of its markings. Pot when new roots emerge from the base of the developing growth.

**Right:** *Pot.* Aztec's Red Beauty 'Aztec' HCC/AOS. The fiery tones seen here are not easily achieved, but orchid breeders continue to try to lock in such rich colors. The breeding lines seen here, originating in *Blc.* Oconee, do not always give the easiest plants to grow. However, as long as the grower observes proper potting practices, dividing and potting only when new roots are present, good results can be assured. Standard plants grow to 18" (46 cms) tall with three to four 6" (15 cms) blooms.

**Left:** *Epi. ciliare* 'Puddle Jumper' FCC/AOS. This is a very easy-to-grow species in the *Cattleya* group, often overlooked owing to the prosaic nature of the color. However, superior clones do show up from time to time, as with 'Puddle Jumper', and growers always take notice. Available from nurseries specializing in species orchids, this type does well under a variety of conditions, including outdoors in frost-free areas. Plants reach 24" (61 cms) at maturity and prefer to be slightly underpotted in a cattleya mix.

# Vandaceous and Angraecoid orchids

## Winter Care for Vandaceous and Angraecoid orchids

**Light:** Provide all possible light to the plants to make up for short days and poor light quality. This will ensure proper ripening of growth and strong flower stems.

**Temperature:** Avoid exposing to temperatures below 60°Fahrenheit (16°Celsius), even at night.

**Water:** Water with care during short, cool days; water early in the day to allow foliage to dry.

**Fertilizer:** Low nitrogen encourages maximum flower potential.

**Watch for:** Slow drying of mix and diseases caused by stale conditions.

Warmer climate orchids, such as the vandaceous and angraecoid types, are not well represented in the cooler winter months. This makes sense because the plants rarely encounter such near dormancy in their native habitats. The spring months will see a flush of flowering from these, although both *Angcm. eburneum* and *Angcm. sesquipedale* are regular winter bloomers. *Angcm. eburneum* is too large for anything but a greenhouse or subtropical patio, while *Angcm. sesquipedale*, the Star of Bethlehem orchid, is more compact and viable in a windowsill situation. Vandas, on the other hand, rarely make for a good houseplant and almost always require the heat, light, and humidity that only a greenhouse or tropical setting can provide.

In the winter months, only the more uncommon species, such as *V. insignis*, are likely to be seen. Vandaceous types

**Left:** *Angcm. eburneum* 'Carol' AM/AOS. One of the best known of this African genus, *Angcm. eburneum* is a plant that requires lots of room to grow. Plants may reach a height of 3" (8 cms) and be equally wide. Suits warmth and moderate light. Keep moist and pot infrequently. This example is seed-raised from a cross between two different forms of this variable species, resulting in a superior form.

**Above:** *Angcm. sesquipedale*, Darwin's Orchid! The specific name *sesquipedale* means one and a half feet, and refers to the length of the spur. Darwin postulated, correctly, that there must be a moth with a proboscis long enough to reach the bottom of the spur. Plants are 18–24" (46–61 cms) tall and equally broad, with robust white roots. Suits warm conditions and moderate shade.

Left: *Aranda* Noorah Alsagoff. This type of vandaceous hybrid is popular both as a cut flower and a potted plant. It flowers freely throughout the year in tropical areas of the world. In less tropical climates, it requires a warm and humid greenhouse to coax flowers from the often tall, to 48" (1.2 meters) or more, plants. Best grown in a slatted basket to allow copious watering and infrequent potting. This plant will perform well in the southern areas of the U.S. Often available from suppliers based in south Florida.

have been widely bred as cut-flowers in Southeast Asia, where year round tropical conditions allow for year round flowering. One may, therefore, occasionally encounter one or another of this type for sale, such as *Aranda*. Noorah Alsagoff. These are most often seen in South Florida, where they are imported as cuttings, often in spike.

*Rhynchostylis gigantea*, from Thailand, is sure to make a splashy presentation with its cascading foxtails of medium size blooms in January and February. Moderately sized, except when allowed to grow into a specimen plants, this species has been popular since the late 1960s. A concentrated effort by Thai breeders resulted in a broad array of color forms, including red, pure white, heavily spotted, and more recently, a near peach color.

**Left:** *V. insignis* 'Mary Motes' AM/AOS. This highly improved species demonstrates the value of continued inbreeding in the production of more attractive flowers. Little used in breeding until quite recently, it's only now becoming more available. Plants seem to do best under typical *Vanda* conditions of high heat and humidity, where they may flower throughout the year, including winter. Stems bear four to eight 3" (8 cms) blooms with unusually large lips.

**Right:** *Rhy. gigantea*. The "Foxtail Orchid" from Thailand is highly popular and very prized in winter for its luxurious plume-like flower stems. Its 2" (5 cms) blooms may be pure white, white with spots or blotches, or pure red. There are even peach tones available now. Plants stay rather short, to 12" (30 cms), but attain large size by basal branching to over 2" (5 cms) across. Flowers appear on two to four stems per growth, and are fragrant during the day. Best grown in slatted baskets where the thick, rambling roots do not have to be disturbed too often. Widely available in the specialist trade and at early spring orchid shows.

# Dendrobiums

Dendrobiums are not commonly seen in winter months. Despite the size of the genus—one of the largest of all orchid genera at 1000 or more species—only a few species and hybrids flower during northern hemisphere winter. These include deciduous types that flower from the nodes of mature canes, such as *Den. constrictum* and *epidendroides*. *Den. constrictum*, particularly, has very long-lasting blooms as is common with higher-elevation plants. *Den. peguanum* is a charming miniature that is just becoming more commonly available thanks to the efforts of Hawaiian nurserymen. These unusual dendrobiums are not commonly seen in retail outlets, but are worth searching out at orchid shows and specialty orchid vendors on-line. The advantage of these three plants is that they are all rather compact, therefore more suited for indoor culture than most. Also, since they are winter dormant, they are more easily accommodated indoors while they are not actively growing. And, of course, their winter flowering brightens up an otherwise green space in your growing area.

Don't forget that deciduous orchids show their blooms off a bit better because the flowers are not obscured by foliage. A great example of this is *Den. anosmum*, which flowers all along the pendant, deciduous canes. *Den. anosmum* is popularly known as "Hono Hono" in Hawaii, where it is widely propagated as a garden plant. This species is prized not only for its lovely blooms, but also for its enchanting fragrance. Also seen are the cane-type dendrobiums, such as *Den.* Mickey Parker, which, because they have been specifically bred as potted plants, tend to flower throughout the year.

**Right:** *Den.* Mickey Parker. Typical of modern Den Phals, *Den.* Mickey Parker is a tall plant, growing to over 30" (76 cms). It can be top-heavy and is best displayed in a heavy cachepot. Growers in warm areas do best with this type as it requires all the light, warmth and heat available during the summer months to do its best. It is not a good houseplant. While growing, it should be given copious water and fertilizer to enable it to make best use of favorable conditions. The deeply colored flowers are long lasting (over four weeks in the home) and can be found in a broad range of colors. This type is widely available.

**Left:** *Den. peguanum*. This miniature hails from India, Thailand and Burma. It grows as a lithophyte or epiphyte and is characterized by short, stout pseudobulbs. Many small fragrant flowers are produced on leafless canes in winter. When not in growth, water should be reduced and fertilizer eliminated. Provide bright filtered light and warm to intermediate temperatures.

**Far left:** *Den. constrictum*. In the pedilonum section of the genus *Dendrobium*, the flowers are very long-lasting, sometimes for two months or more. This species is found in New Guinea and other nearby islands. In cultivation it requires warm to intermediate temperatures and year-round watering. This species can be grown under lights or in the window, as it is rather small.

# CYMBIDIUMS

Cymbidiums—the darlings of West Coast growers because they thrive in outdoor gardens there—are traditionally a spring-blooming plant. Sadly, most cymbidiums will only flower in areas where the summer night temperatures do not rise much above 60°Fahrenheit (16°Celsius), so the Pacific coast is where they do best. However, over the past 20 years, breeders have endeavored to extend the flowering season back into winter and fall months and also to impart greater warmth tolerance by breeding with Asian species.

The result is a new population of warmth-tolerant, earlier blooming cyms. The color range is still rather limited, but brightly hued examples such as *Cym.* Golden Vanguard demonstrate how showy this new breed can be. Flower life is not as long as standard cymbidiums, which can often stretch for four or more weeks, but the shorter bloom period is compensated for by intense perfume. Interestingly, the smaller flowers often have the more intense perfume and may also have more intense color, as in *Cym.* Nut.

---

**Right:** *Cym.* Nut is a compact cymbidium with slender foliage that seldom exceeds 30" (76 cms). Upright stems of six to ten blooms are borne in early winter. Best results are achieved where the plant can be summered outdoors. Keep evenly moist.

---

**Far right:** *Cym.* Golden Vanguard 'New Horizon' HCC/AOS. Hybrids from the tetraploid, improved form of *Cym.* Golden Elf lead the way in smaller-growing and more tolerant cymbidiums. Traditional cymbidiums require cool nights in late summer to flower, but those with Asian species in their background do not. Add in the petite foliage and brilliant yellow color, and you have an outstanding early winter display. Grow as for *Cym.* Nut, with very bright light and lots of water during the growing season.

# PHAIUS HYBRIDS

Closely related to cymbidiums, *Phaius* species and hybrids are becoming increasingly popular as garden plants in the southern and Gulf Coast states. Best known for the stately *Phaius tankervilleae*, the 'Nun's Orchid,' this group shows very large and robust growth with long and broad leaves. The inflorescences rise from the newly developing growths in midwinter and are in glorious bloom by late January into February.

A more traditional phaius "look" is demonstrated by *Phaius* Micro Burst, showing the attractive mahogany petals and sepals nicely offset by a dark rose lip. As this group has become more popular, breeders have sought to extend the range of colors by the use of other related genera and species, exemplified by *Gsph*. Kitty Crocker, a bright-yellow flower borne on a more compact plant.

Because of their size and need for large pots of terrestrial mix, phaius are really only suited for frost-free areas. They thrive in a sunroom or enclosed patio where their large size can be easily accommodated. Commercial growers have found that phaius grow rapidly under the right conditions, so you are likely to be tempted by these plants in spike at your local garden center. Fortunately, the price is often reasonable enough to justify a purchase simply for the flowers, much as you would buy a poinsettia or chrysanthemum. Otherwise, these plants need strong light, good humidity, and even moisture.

---

**Left:** *Gsph*. Kitty Crocker 'Newberry' HCC/AOS. While technically a *Gastrophaius, Gastrochilus* x *Phaius*, most will consider this a phaius. Unlike most orchids, phaius do better in slightly larger pots. Give copious water and fertilizer while in active growth. Warm and bright conditions suit these best.

---

**Right:** *Phaius*. Micro Burst 'Orchtober Fest' AM/AOS. Bred by crossing a smaller growing species with the majestic *Phaius tankervilleae*, Micro Burst has the attributes of its large parent on a more manageable plant. Suits bright light and high humidity.

# PAPHIOPEDILUMS

The Lady Slipper orchids, the Old World paphiopedilums and the New World phragmipediums, flower throughout the year. Typically, each season has its distinct types which characterize that time of year, and winter is no exception. The hybrids resulting from the newly discovered Chinese paphs represent a new look in slippers, as shown in *Paph.* Lynleigh Koopowitz. This type of hybrid, owing to the relative rarity of the parental stock coupled with the value conferred by their recent introduction makes these more difficult to find in typical retail outlets. Interested growers must search these out.

The multiflora paphs, such as *Paph.* Julius, have long been the realm of the connoisseur because they are generally slow growing and difficult to flower, owing to their *Paph. rothschildianum* parent.

Because nursery-bred roths have been improved to grow

**Left:** *Paph*. Delrosi is notorious for being one of the most difficult paphs to bloom. Growers must patiently allow the plants to reach mature growth, which may take ten years or more. Bright light and light fertilization suit this plant best. Seven-inch (18 cms) blooms are borne two or three to a 12" (30 cms) stem and are definitely worth the wait.

**Above:** *Paph*. Lynleigh Koopowitz 'Krull Smith' FCC/AOS. One of the earliest hybrids to utilize the recently discovered Chinese species, *Paph. malipoense*, this is a lovely and easy-to-grow orchid. Grows well with phals or with catts if more shade can be provided. Keep evenly moist. The creamy white blooms may have a light fragrance during the day.

**Right:** *Paph.* Julius 'Crownfox' AM/AOS. Raised in astounding numbers for this type of strap-leaf hybrid and therefore widely known and grown, *Paph.* Julius may be the easiest of this type to flower. Tall stems, to more than 30" (76 cms), bear three to five "flying" blooms of 7" (18 cms) or more. Plants may be 30" (76 cms) or more wide. They appreciate bright light and intermediate temperatures.

quickly and flower easily, more and more of the multiflora types have entered the market. While the Chinese species and hybrids are proving to respond to more typical paph culture, the multifloras, which are also known as "strap leaf" for their long leaves, require care that is quite different. They need higher light, slightly drier conditions at the roots, and more care with fertilization.

None of the paphs are particularly heavy feeders and these are no exception, although they will respond to higher fertilizer rates than many other paphs. The key to flowering strap-leaf types seems to be a reduction or elimination of fertilizer during winter months to trigger mature growths into flower. One of the frustrating aspects of multiflora culture is that it often takes two or three years to mature a new growth to flowering size. Paphs in general do best if left to grow into larger, multiple growth plants before division.

# PANSIES AND LYCASTES

Two groups that begin to flower in winter months are the lycastes and the Colombian miltonias or miltoniopsis, which are also known under the collective name of Pansy orchids. While the first of these begin to bloom in winter, they are more commonly associated with spring.

Colombian *Miltonia* such as *Milt. vexillaria* and closely related hybrids like *Milt.* Second Love herald the beginning of the flowering season for this fine group of orchids. Unfortunately, these are not the easiest orchids to grow because their love of constantly moderate temperatures and good quality water is not easily duplicated outside of areas like the Pacific Northwest where it naturally occurs.

*Lycaste* is a large genus of orchids roughly divided into deciduous, or those that drop their leaves in winter, and non-deciduous types. The first of the deciduous types begin to bloom during the winter, providing a flush of flowers from the base of the mature growth with each flower borne singly on an upright stem.

*Lyc. macrobulbon* (shown on the facing page) is one of the showiest of the genus and may bear a dozen or more individual flowers from the base of the new growth. Deciduous lycastes, like many other orchids that rest during the late fall and winter months, should not be watered during leafless months. Wait until the new growth is well advanced and root growth has commenced. Plants not allowed to enter into dormancy may flower poorly or not at all.

---

**Right top:** *Milt. vexillaria* Leucoglossa – 'Leucoglossa' means "white lipped," denoting the unusual white lip of this normally pink lipped species from Colombia. Grow under mild conditions with cool nights and days, using good quality water. Do not overpot.

---

**Right bottom:** *Milt.* Second Love 'Tokimeki' AM/AOS – Basically a highly improved form of *Milt. vexillaria*, this fine hybrid demonstrates the quality of modern breeding. Grow as you do the species. Available from specialty nurseries.

# OTHER WINTER-FLOWERING ORCHIDS

While there is a relative wealth of flowering candidates in the more familiar groups of orchids, there is also a bounty of unusual, one of a kind and botanical orchids that flower in winter. The South African species *Bonatea speciosa* is a wonderful example of this type. It is also a good example of how nursery propagation can successfully reduce pressure on natural populations. This plant is such a fast and robust grower under good conditions that one southern California nursery has been able to produce literally hundreds of plants each year from divisions.

**Below:** *Cycds*. Jem's Blood Ruby is an unusual intergeneric hybrid made from *Cycnoches* and *Mormodes*. The plants are moderately sized, up to 18" (46 cms), with broad, palm-like leaves that are deciduous in the winter. The richly colored blooms appear on horizontal stems that emerge from the leaf axils. Grow under cattleya conditions.

**Right:** *Bonatea speciosa* is a wonderful terrestrial that grows near the beach, in sandy soil, in South Africa. Robust tubers produce upright leafy stems topped with heads of swan-like, perfumed, 2" (5 cms) blooms. Rest in winter after growths have died back. Water and fertilize heavily as growths emerge in late winter.

**Left:** *Bulbophyllum grandiflorum* is a unique member of this large genus. Sometimes seen as *Hyalosema*, this is a warm-growing plant from low elevations. Grow under phalaenopsis conditions, keeping constantly moist in a shallow pan to accommodate the long rhizomes. Its bizarre blooms are large and can grow to over 6" (15 cms).

**Right:** *Dinema polybulbon* is a dwarf member of the cattleya alliance. It is ideal for under lights or windowsill growing where the tiny—under 4" (10 cms)—growths quickly fill a pot in an attractive way. Bright light and even moisture will allow the plant to produce the single-flowered stems from the apex of the growths.

*Bonatea* is deciduous, with growth beginning in January and showy, fragrant egret-like blooms coming as early as February. The deciduous New World orchids in the *Cycnoches* and *Mormodes* group are another winter standout, with *Cycds*. Jem's Blood Ruby a wonderful example of the rich, deep colors and exotic flower shapes possible in this group.

Like *Dendrobium*, *Bulbophyllum* is a very large and widespread genus of more than 1,000 species. Because it occurs in nature from sea level to high elevation, and from the equator to higher latitudes, there are bulbophyllums for every season. Winter sees examples from the large-flowered *Bulb. grandiflorum* to the smaller but more profusely flowered *Bulb. orientale*.

The New World counterparts to the widely distributed bulbophyllums are the pleurothallids, such as *Pleurothallis*, *Masdevallia*, and others. There is a multitude of species available from specialty sources. These are popular under-lights and windowsill orchids in the Northeast where their compact nature and love of cooler conditions make them ideal for the cool climates found there.

And there are simply those orchids that do not comfortably fit into any group, such as *Dinema polybulbon*, long known as an *Epidendrum*, and *Cischweinfia rostrata*. Both of these compact growers make great indoor orchids that quickly provide a profuse floral display in a small space. Finally, and while they are not grown for their flowers, are the jewel orchids, such as *Ludisia discolor*, which make an elegant flowering subject in winter while providing lovely year-round foliage.

---

**Below:** *Ludisia discolor*, the archetypal jewel orchid, produces lovely displays of white blooms under good conditions. Normally grown in deep shade to preserve the foliar markings, a bit more light will bring forth the upright flower stems. Keep evenly moist and shady in intermediate to warm conditions.

# SPRING-FLOWERING ORCHIDS

*Spring is a time of growth and the best opportunity to repot your orchid. It is also the time when a host of cattleyas come into bloom.*

## SPRING CARE

### GENERAL

**Day length:** Increases significantly and plants often begin growth cycle.

**Light:** Becomes stronger as sun rises higher in sky. Watch for burning on foliage that is soft from winter growth. Changeable conditions require close observation.

**Temperatures:** Rise as the days become warmer. However, nights remain cool and temperature fluctuation can be difficult for plants. Danger of frost decreases further south.

**Overall:** Almost all plants will respond with new growth or increasing growth rate; some flowering initiated from growth ripened over winter.

### GROWER RESPONSE

**Watering:** Increase frequency to once a week or more often as season progresses, as indicated by plant root growth and increasing rapidity of drying.

**Fertilizer:** Half strength at every watering, alternated with clear water every fourth watering.

**Watch for:** New growths, new roots, new flower stems and/or buds. Changing light conditions dictate close observation and quick response by grower.

Spring is the season that has been called the time of quickening. The plants begin to respond to longer days, better light quality, and higher temperatures with rapidly increasing growth rates. Orchids are often thought to be rather slow-growing plants and this is generally true, but in the spring it is not. Plants are spurred into growth and many types often make their entire year's growth in the few months of spring and summer.

Many types rush to flower, stimulated by a reaction to factors that, in their native habitats, would indicate the beginning of the time most favorable to nutrient-draining seed production and germination. This is also a time when pollinators are newly active and flowers are most attractive. Days grow longer and the sun grows more powerful as it rises higher above the horizon. Temperatures rise naturally with the increased quality and duration of light, and the ground begins to warm, resulting in higher night temperatures as well. All of these factors and more trigger orchids into a growth spurt.

Observant growers know what to look for during this season and are quick to provide their plants with the increased water and fertilizer they will require to optimize their growth during this critical period. Plants that have simply held on during dark winter months begin to perk up, making new growth and initiating roots. Increasing metabolic rates and rising temperatures make media dry more rapidly, signaling the need for more frequent watering.

### Spring Maintenance

Spring is also when necessary dividing and repotting is best carried out. When observant growers select the time of potting judiciously, based on the known rooting behavior

**Right:** *C. mossiae* coerulea is a unifoliate (one leaf per pseudobulb) cattleya species that comes in a variety of color forms. It is native to Venezuela and blooms in late spring. Plants are generally less than 24" (61 cms) and may bear six or seven 8" (20 cms) blooms. The species is recognized by the season and by the dark, veined lip.

of the particular plant, setback is minimized, and the plant will often continue in growth with little if any adverse effect. The new roots will grow into the fresh medium, ready to support the emerging growth. Winter flowering plants with remaining flowers will often benefit from the removal of persistent blooms to allow needed repotting.

With potting comes cleaning. Plants should be inspected for pests that have overwintered, and the pests removed. Remove any diseased portions. Growers should begin to ready their plants for a move outdoors after the threat of frost is past to make maximum use of good growing time. Fertilization should be gradually increased during the spring months to coincide with increased need.

### Show Time

Spring is the most popular season for orchid shows throughout the United States. Historically, spring is the season when most orchid cut flowers have been sold and so it became the best time for growers to trot out their wares and show off. People were the most receptive to orchid flowers and in the mood to purchase after a cold, dreary winter.

While orchid shows happen throughout the year, in recent times the main concentration has been in the months of February through May. This has driven growers to select plants that flower during these months. Thus more flowering plants are available, so hobbyists can see more flowers at shows. This has created more interest in shows, driving more show-oriented sales of spring-flowering stock, and so on.

The lesson is that both by design and by accident, spring will tend to be the season in which a high proportion of your plants tend to flower. This is not a bad thing because spring-flowering orchids tend to be somewhat more amenable to bad conditions during winter months, owing to a semi-dormancy. They are popular plants because everyone appreciates some cheering up after a long, dark winter.

---

**Below:** *Paph.* William Ambler 'Jim Krull' AM/AOS. Closely resembling its *Paph. rothschildianum* parent, this striking hybrid is more compact than the species, with growths that may only reach 24" (61 cms). As with other strap-leaf hybrids, this plant requires more light and heat than many slippers, and does best when grown into large, multigrowth plants. The tall flower stems will bear three or four stately blooms that may reach 10" (25 cms) or more across.

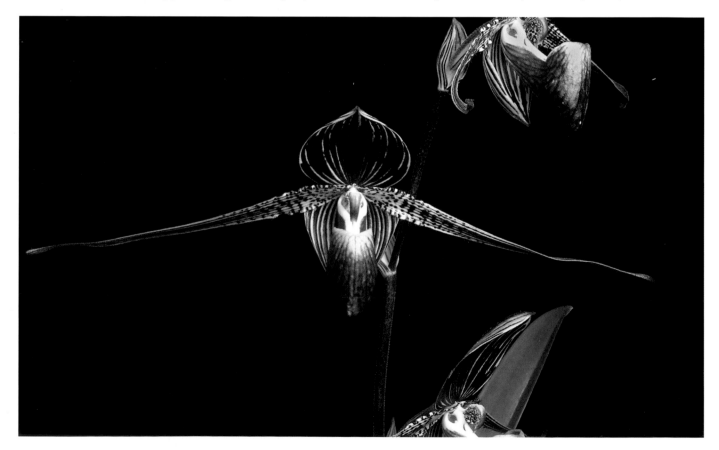

**Right:** *Inobulbon munificum* is recognized, even when not in flower, by its stout, hairy pseudobulbs that are between 8" (20 cms) and 10" (25 cms) tall. The flower stems emerge horizontally from the leaf axils on the pseudobulbs and branch to produce dozens of 2" (5 cms) blooms. This is a slow-growing orchid, seldom offered in the trade but worth searching out. Requires warmth and shade.

# CATTLEYAS

## SPRING CARE FOR CATTLEYAS

**Light:** Increasing day length and light intensity trigger new growth and flower production.

**Water:** Increase watering in response to quicker drying of medium and to faster plant metabolism.

**Fertilizer:** Increase frequency and concentration to match watering and plant needs.

**Watch for:** Rapid pest build up, which is likely under favorable conditions; flower stem initiation. Stake inflorescences as they grow.

Cattleyas are in their glory in the spring months. There is such a wealth of beauty that it is difficult to know where to begin. Because this bounty occurred naturally at a time when orchids were in high demand, perhaps no other orchid was more heavily exploited during the Victorian era of orchid growing.

This trend has followed through to modern times. Consumers are especially interested in orchids in spring months, as the dull winter days begin to wane. They think of cattleyas as quintessential orchids. Cattleya flowers have been the traditional flower for spring holidays such as Easter and Mother's Day. Production ramped up for these

**Right:** *Lc. Canhamiana* 'Azure Skies' AM/AOS was first registered in 1885 and it is one of the earliest examples of a primary intergeneric (two or more genera combined). It has since been remade many times, most recently in the blue, or coerulea, form. This was a happy marriage because the plants have been very floriferous and easy to grow as well as relatively compact for type—under 20" (51 cms) tall. Grow as for other cattleyas.

**Left:** *C. mossiae* venosa 'Canaima's Mercedes' HCC/AOS is another of the many distinct color varieties discovered in its native Venezuela. Venosa is characterized by the strong veining in the lip and the slight flaring of darker color in the petals. Provide regular fertilization and allow to dry between waterings. Slightly cooler temperatures during winter help to produce more flowers, as does strong light during the growing season.

two holidays resulted in a good supply of traditional cattleyas that normally flower in this season.

Typically, the traditional spring flowering cattleyas bloom from the previous season's growth, which has been in sheath since the preceding autumn. With lengthening days, the bud primordia encased in the sheath responds by activating and developing into a strong flowering stem. *C. lueddemanniana* is an early spring bloomer, often coming in as early as late February and into March. This lovely Venezuelan species, recognizable by its unusual diamond-dust sparkle and veined lip, was once uncommon.

Today, we are seeing an increasing number of fine, highly bred examples coming in from its country of origin as well as from domestic breeders.

Like most seasonal cattleya species, *C. lueddemanniana* can be a bit picky about when it is potted. If it is not potted when roots are active, it may not do well for a year or more until new roots initiate. Generally, the best time to pot for this type is immediately after flowering, before the new growth emerges. It is interesting to note that the conventional wisdom is to pot when the new growth comes. This can be the most awkward time, owing to the

difficulty of avoiding breakage of the new growth, as well as the fact that the rooting may not come until substantially later in the growth cycle.

Closely related to *C. lueddemanniana*, and much better known, is *C. mossiae*. This lovely species is the progenitor of all of our best spring lavender colors. Highly selected forms from Venezuela are still among the most beautiful and striking of all cattleyas.

Like most of its unifoliate cousins, *C. mossiae*'s typical color form is lavender, complemented by white, semi-alba (white with colored lip), and coerulea (blue) forms. The recent availability of improved forms of these well-known species has engendered a new interest in the reproduction of classic cattleya primary hybrids. *C. trimoss* was first made in the late nineteenth century, but retains a beauty and charm that newer hybrids cannot often match.

*Lc. canhamiana* is another remake of a primary hybrid from the dawn of cattleya hybridizing that has made its mark on today's orchid scene. One of the traits that makes this type most attractive is the hybrid vigor that enables them to grow exceptionally easily and produce a bounty of flowers from compact plants.

Along with the unifoliate species comes a broad and scintillating array of standard, large flowered cattleya hybrids. These range in color from the rose lavender of *Bc.* Esther Peters, to the golden yellows of *Blc.* Malworth and *Blc.* Bill Krull, through the chartreuse of *Blc.* Nina de Borinquen and *Blc.* Yueng Kang-Sen, and finally to the brilliant sunset tones of fine plants like *Blc.* Pete Harry.

Types of orchid that bear inclusion with the standard cattleyas are the hybrids from *C. walkeriana*. Though technically a bifoliate, *C. walkeriana* has the aspect of a smaller growing unifoliate, with flowers that are proportionately large for the diminutive plant size. *C. walkeriana* is exceptionally valuable as a parent because it is dominant for plant size while allowing the flowers to

**Left:** *C. trimoss* represents a remake of one of the earliest of all cattleya hybrids. This superior example shows the improved form and brilliant color imparted by better-quality parents. *C. trimoss* is a seminal parent, showing up in the bloodlines of many cut-flower hybrids. Plants may be a little large, but flower freely under normal cattleya conditions.

**Top right:** *Blc.* Nina de Borinquen "Irma la Douche" AM/AOS. This more recent hybrid shows the strong influence of its species parent, *Brassavola digbyana*, seen in the heavily fringed lip. While the flower count per growth is lower than many cattleyas, owing to the single-flowered species parent, the brilliance of color, fragrance, and long-lasting qualities more than make up for any shortfalls in number of flowers. This type of cattleya does best in strong light and warm conditions.

**Bottom right:** *Blc.* Malworth 'Orchidglade' FCC/AOS is a famous and highly awarded hybrid that was once the standard by which all yellow cattleyas were judged. Today, it retains its worth as a beautiful and easy-to-grow example of type. Plants are large, to 24" (61 cms) or more, and strong growing, with no particular idiosyncrasies.

**Above:** *Lc.* Crownfox
Sweetheart 'Crownfox'
HCC/AOS. Line breeding with
the small growing species *C.
walkeriana* produces flowers
that are proportionately quite
large. Dry between waterings
and give strong light.

**Left:** *C. granulosa* 'Canaima'
AM/AOS is a moderately sized
bifoliate (two to four leaves per
pseudobulb) cattleya, which
grows to about 30" (76 cms)
and bears four to six 5" (13
cms) blooms. Its spade-shaped
lip characterizes the species. Pot
when new roots emerge and
allow to dry between waterings.

remain relatively large and shapely. Progeny such as *Lc.* Mem. Robert Strait and *Lc.* Crownfox Sweetheart are exemplary of the fine, easy-to-grow results of this type of breeding.

This type is outstanding for home culture because its smaller size is more easily accommodated on the windowsill or under lights and the large flowers can nearly obscure the plant.

As the season progresses toward summer, more and

**Below:** *C. skinneri* is one of the most prolific bifoliate cattleyas and is very popular for spring bloom, particularly in areas where it grows best, such as south Florida. Plants are 20" (51 cms) tall and have clusters of rose-lavender 3" (8 cms) blooms. Best results are obtained when allowed to grow into a large specimen.

more bifoliate (two or more leaves per growth) species and hybrids come into flower. Prominent among the species are *C. amethystoglossa*, *C. aclandiae*, *C. aurantiaca*, *C. skinneri* and *C. granulosa*. Each has its special charms, and each has its place both as a fine flower in its own right as well as the progenitor of a type of hybrid.

Least utilized, but perhaps most singularly beautiful, is *C. amethystoglossa*. This species has been the subject of intense specialist interest, which has resulted in some highly improved forms. *C. aclandiae* is a dwarf species with boldly marked blooms. This species does best mounted unconstrained by medium, to allow its fat roots to ramble freely. Breeders use it for both its distinct markings as well as its compact growth habit. Interestingly, it was one of the parents of the first hybrid cattleya to bloom, *C. Brabantiae*.

Modern remakes of this hybrid have given highly improved and very popular forms.

Cattleya aclandiae is also popular as the sire of a race of fine reds resulting from Slc. Precious Stones. As a parent, the Central American species C. aurantiaca needs no introduction. An entire subtype of multiflora orange cattleyas, including Lc. Trick or Treat, has resulted from C. aurantiaca. This species has also been highly bred by specialist nurseries, yielding a variety of color forms from white through yellow and pink as well as highly improved standard orange forms.

Cattleya aurantiaca and C. skinneri originate in the same area of Central America and often interbreed to form the highly variable C. Guatemalensis. This natural hybrid forms what are known as swarms where the hybrids interbreed with each other, as well as with each of the two species parents, to form a population of highly unusual flower forms and colors. C. skinneri has not been widely used as a parent but is one of the most popular spring specimen plants, owing to the ease with which large plants covered with blooms are produced.

In South Florida, spring shows are sometimes literally awash in large, many-flowered plants of this species. While the typical color form of C. skinneri is sparkling rose-lavender, coerulea (blue) forms are also in the trade. C. granulosa is less common than the rest of this group, but is important as the species that gave us many of our modern green cattleya hybrids through its use in Lc. Ethel Merman.

An interesting byway to green cattleya breeding, involving C. granulosa background, may be seen in Eplc. Mae Bly. All bifoliate cattleyas are highly seasonal in their growth and consequently, great care must be taken when they are repotted. All root at different stages of their growth cycle, so the grower must closely observe the habits of any given species or hybrid. Over a period of several years, the grower will learn when the best time to repot occurs. Later in the season, bifoliate whites derived from C. loddigesii and C. intermedia begin to bloom, as seen in C. Henrietta Japhet.

Concentrating on these two well-known groups may give the false impression that these are the only types of cattleyas in bloom in spring months. Nothing could be further from the truth. Spring has the greatest variety of cattleyas of any season.

Minicatts originating from the Brazilian species Soph.

**Top left:** *C.* Brabantiae 'Palm Sunday' is one of the earliest artificial hybrids. Registered in 1863, *C.* Brabantiae has enjoyed resurgence in popularity as it has been remade with superior examples of the species parents. Rich rose-pink color and heavy substance mark 'Palm Sunday'. *C.* Brabantiae makes a good houseplant cattleya owing to its compact—8–10" (20–25 cms)— stature and easy-going nature. Give bright light and regular fertilizer and allow to dry between waterings.

**Bottom left:** With *C. granulosa* as a grandparent and the green Mexican species *Epi. mariae* as a parent, it is no wonder that the green of this *Eplc.* Mae Bly is especially vivid. No taller than 10" (25 cms), plants give two or three good-sized blooms that may be 4" (10 cms) across. Easy to grow on the windowsill or in the greenhouse, *Eplc.* Mae Bly has been remade several times, so is usually available from a variety of specialist suppliers.

**Right:** *C.* Henrietta Japhet is the first of its type. Multiflora white cattleyas, 'Japhets' are easy to grow. Flowering twice a year, these were once a standard cut flower, along with primary hybrids like *C.* Claesiana. Of moderate height, to 28" (71 cms), the bifoliate growth gives five to eight 4" (10 cms) blooms two or three times per year.

**Above:** *Blc.* Rustic Spots 'O'Whimsey' AM/AOS. Hybrids based in *Brassavola nodosa* are deservedly popular. They tend to do well in areas that are too warm for regular cattleyas. Plants are compact, to 15" (38 cms) or so, and are easy to grow. They can cover themselves with blooms multiple times in each year.

**Opposite top:** *Osmt.* Richard Fulford 'Mem. Loretta Carlson' AM/AOS is a complex intergeneric that embodies the best qualities of *Broughtonia* breeding. Usually under 8" (20 cms), they have upright stems of 12 or more brilliantly colored blooms to 2" (5 cms). Prolific and freely branching, they may flower multiple times in each year.

*coccinea* are at their best, as with *Slc.* Dream Catcher. It is now that we see the first of the highly popular line of hybrids from the Lady of the Night orchid, *B. nodosa. Blc.* Rustic Spots shows the characteristic charm of this type, which not only tends to be quite easy to grow and flowers even in the warmest areas but also retains a species-like beauty shared by few others.

The Caribbean species *Broughtonia sanguinea* is at its best during this period, as are its hybrids. *Bro. sanguinea*

has been discovered in a variety of color forms, and is the sire of a race of very compact hybrids such as *Osmt.* Richard Fulford. Very shapely blooms and flat lips, borne on strong upright stems, characterize *Bro. sanguinea* and its hybrids. *Bro. sanguinea* hybrids can quickly morph far from their species progenitor, as seen in *Otr.* IIwa Yuan Bay—a dazzling splash petal type bred from *Lctna.* Peggy San. Brazilian laelias and encyclias also begin to come into their own during this season.

**Right:** *Otra*. Hwa Yuan Bay 'She Shu' is another complex intergeneric with five genera included. The *Broughtonia* influence dwarfs the plant while giving brightly colored flowers of heavy substance. The plants may be no more than 6" (15 cms) tall with 10" (25 cms) stems of round, 2" (5 cms), flared beauties. Keep in a relatively small pot to help avoid over watering.

An especially nice and increasingly common species is *Enc. bractescens*, which, owing to its very compact nature, makes a fine specimen plant in as little as a 4 inch (10 cms) pot. With floriferous and colorful hybrids like *Eplc.* Orange Crush, *Eplc.* Rojorufa and *Scl.* Newberry Lava Burst becoming more frequently available in markets, it is easy to see how their popularity is on the increase.

A more unusual color combination is seen in *Yam.* Saint Thomas, an ethereally beautiful green. The best feature of all of these plants is that they are very easy to grow. Because they are almost entirely dormant, with very little growth, they overwinter in the home with little harm, ready to burst into bloom at the first sign of spring's benefits. Additionally, they tend to be very fast growing under commercial conditions, allowing growers to bring them to market in good time.

For the more dedicated grower, more obscure cattleya alliance species can also provide a lot of interest. *Caularthron* (aka *Diacrium*) *bicornutum* is one of the most attractive white species, and has given rise to a race of beautiful *Diacattleya* and *Dialaelia* hybrids, known for their exceptional lasting quality. *Leptotes bicolor* is a little known Brazilian species worth searching out both for its proportionately large blooms and its terete growth habit.

*Hexisea bidentata* is very seldom seen, and even less often well grown but compensates for any difficulty with its rich orange blooms. The widespread and variable epidendrums are well represented with the unusual *Epi. stamfordianum*, which produces its branching (uncommon in epidendrums) inflorescence from the base of the mature bulb, which is unique in the genus. This species is an outstanding subject for basket culture in warmer climates.

Another avenue of cattleya-alliance breeding that has recently been rekindled is that of reedstem epidendrums. This colorful and easy-to-grow group is a staple of frost free gardens from California to Hawaii to Florida, where they thrive in nearly full sun to partial shade. Their drawbacks include a limited color range in the orange tones and a large, rambling growth habit that is difficult to contain in pots.

Enterprising breeders have created a new race of these combines a much richer palette of colors ranging from nearly white through pink, lavender, reds, oranges and yellow, with a more compact and upright growth habit. Whether or not they will be as cold-tolerant as their forebears remains to be seen. There are also breeders concentrating on producing the darkest possible reds, as seen in *Epi.* Hokulea.

**Right:** Similar to *Eplc.* Rojorufa, *Eplc.* Orange Crush has larger blooms on a slightly larger plant, owing to the size of both parents. The plants will attain a height of 24" (61 cms) and have tall, upright spikes of brilliant orange stars. This is another good plant for the frost-free garden. Hawaiian nurseries occasionally offer these.

**Left:** *Eplc.* Rojorufa 'KG's Sunburst Gibson' JC/AOS. Not all hybridizing is done by large nurseries. Experienced hobbyist growers often make insightful hybrids that are of interest to many more growers than will ever be lucky enough to see them. This cross of the well-known orange-red multiflora *Lc.* Rojo with the seldom seen *Enc. rufa* is a wonderful example of a small-growing plant with big appeal. These will make good garden plants either with cymbidiums or cattleyas.

**Left:** *Leptotes bicolor* is a dwarf—often less than 4" (10 cms) tall—cousin of cattleyas. It has quill-like pendant buds and unusual ivory blooms, to 2" (5 cms), in clusters of two to five. Either slatted wooden baskets or mounts are favored for this species owing to its pendant growth habit. It is a tolerant plant that will do well in the frost-free garden and indoors in a bright window or greenhouse.

**Right:** *Epi.* Hokulea is a modern hybrid in the traditional reedstem group of epis, which are getting progressively shorter. The best stay under 36" (91 cms) in flower, with larger blooms reaching 2" (5 cms) in brilliant shades of red, orange, yellow, and peach. The blooming period of this type lasts for months because the stem will branch much like a phal. These are not good houseplants because they require all the strong light you can provide. The plants are attractive, with canes of opposing rounded leaves. Keep evenly moist and regularly fertilized. Good for the frost-free garden or the greenhouse. Look for these at specialist nurseries and occasionally at garden centers.

# PHALAENOPSIS

## SPRING CARE FOR PHALAENOPSIS

**Light:** Longer days and higher sun angles necessitate closer grower attention to avoid burning winter-softened foliage. As plants become accustomed to higher light, more may be let through.

**Water:** Whether flowering or growing, phals need to be kept evenly moist in spring months, which may mean watering more than once a week, perhaps every four days or so.

**Fertilizer:** Balanced or high nitrogen at full strength, depending on the medium being used.

**Watch for:** Signs of stress induced by media breakdown or excessively high light conditions. Sucking pests such as mealybugs, scale, and aphids can build up very quickly at this time of year.

Phalaenopsis are quite an important feature in the spring palette. However, we begin to see a predominance of those with some *Doritis pulcherrima* background, as these tend to flower a bit later. The *Doritis* is often very far removed in the breeding background of modern hybrids, so far back that the only influence is to make the season a bit more toward spring.

Nevertheless, with new introductions such as *Dtps.* Joy Angel Voice and *Dtps.* Brother Cortez demonstrating modern color possibilities, no one can complain. We also

Below: *Dtps.* Brother Cortez Red 'Caribe' AM/AOS. The spring months are dominated by the novelty-type phals that appear in rich colors and patterns. This type tends to be very long-lasting, often flowering over a period of several months. Red phals are now easily available at garden centers. Plants are typical phalaenopsis, requiring shade, warmth, and regular watering. Keep well fertilized.

see some of the later-blooming types of phalaenopsis, those dominated by *Phal. lueddemanniana* background, such as *Phal.* Fangtastic 'John Curtin'.

Many of the winter-blooming phals are reaching the end of their flowering period by the time May rolls around, and growers must consider whether to allow their spikes to branch for another flowering session or cut the spikes for best summer growth. Larger mature plants are a better candidate for allowing to go a second year in the same mix than are younger, first-bloom plants, as this type can literally flower itself to death if not attended to properly.

**Below:** *Phal.* Fangtastic John Curtin 'Sedona Bright Smile' AM/AOS. Brilliant coalescing red spots over a bright ivory background make this an eye-catcher of the first degree. Look for this type later in the spring almost anywhere phals are sold. The Taiwanese breeders have made this color range very readily available.

# VANDACEOUS ORCHIDS

One of the staples of the spring show season in the southern states, especially in south Florida, is the vandaceous type of orchid. Spring is the season when some of the finest and largest new vanda hybrids are regularly shown. It is also the season to take advantage of improving weather conditions to obtain new plants. This allows them the maximum growing time to acclimatize to your conditions.

Because they hale from such uniformly tropical, warm, and humid climates, vandas can be a challenge for gardeners in more northerly areas. Vandas require all the light, heat, and humidity you can provide. Indeed, vandas love frequent watering so much that the preferred medium in tropical areas is none at all.

The best plants are grown in slatted wooden baskets that allow their roots to freely ramble and give the maximum time between having to disturb them. The downfall of many a vanda has been root damage in potting. Their roots serve as support, and are responsible for water and nutrient uptake. When a vanda loses too many of its roots, it has a difficult time supporting its metabolic needs on the few reserves in its leaves and stem.

For many years, *V. sanderiana* and *V. coerulea* types dominated the market place. This was no bad thing because these two species were responsible for producing the traditional large "platters" beloved of vanda aficionados. Today, we still see improvements in this line of breeding, with such plants as *V.* Adele Graham and *V.* Suzanne Rutzke, among others, leading the pack.

Improved *V. rothschildiana* (*sanderiana* x *coerulea*) types remain popular, owing to their fine blue reticulation, as in *V.* Golamco's Blue Magic and *V.* Nakorn Sawan, which show much *V. coerulea* influence. However, breeders have introduced other vanda species in an attempt to broaden the color range and have succeeded particularly well in creating strong golden yellows based on *V. denisoniana*.

With hybrids like *V.* Golden Dubloon and *V.* Motes Buttercup, yellow vandas are reaching new levels of quality.

**Left:** *V.* Suzanne Rutzke 'Classy Lady' HCC/AOS. Full-size standard vandas take lots of space, along with ample heat and humidity. Best results are attained in the Gulf States and down into south Florida where the warm summers give the plants what they need to perform at their best.

**Above:** *V.* Nakorn Sawan 'Blue Spotty' demonstrates classic blue tessellation that comes through from the species *V. coerulea.* Plants grow to 36" (91 cms) tall and 24" (61 cms) wide, with upright stems of six to a dozen or more 5" (14 cms) blooms. Grow in slatted wooden baskets, with frequent watering and fertilizing. Keep above 65° Fahrenheit (18° Celsius), with days into the 80s or even 90s Fahrenheit (27–37° Celsius).

*V. denisoniana* hybrids have the disadvantage of being very intolerant of cold, tending to lose leaves if night temperatures are allowed to drop to 60–65° Fahrenheit (16–18° Celsius). Unusual colors are also being attempted

with such very dark species as *V. tessellata,* giving midnight colors as in *V.* Pamela Greer, with very saturated pigmentation.

Standard vandas are large plants, and are generally not

**Left:** *V.* Pamela Greer 'Redland Night' AM/AOS. The unusual species *V. tessellata* imparts the stunning dark wine color to this bold flower. As with all vanda types, give plenty of heat, light, and water for best results. Frequently available in the spring months at orchid shows and from specialist vendors.

**Right:** *Ascda.* Freda Hartfield 'Crownfox Gold' HCC/AOS. Brilliant yellow tones are being seen more and more often with the influx of new hybrids from *Asctm. miniatum* and its progeny. Plants are slightly smaller, to 24" (61 cms) or so, but require similar care to other vandas, giving their best in areas such as South Florida. Look for these at specialist growers.

suitable for home growing. Those interested in this style of flower must either have an appropriate greenhouse or live where vandas can be grown outdoors most of the year, such as south Florida and Hawaii. Even where the grower has a greenhouse, vandas are not always the easiest of orchids to grow, especially in more northern areas that are seasonally cool and dark.

Alternatively there is a type of vanda that is more compact and amenable to both greenhouse culture and in some cases, windowsill growing. Ascocendas are the result of crossing the smaller growing and brightly colored species of the genus *Ascocentrum* with standard vandas. Where *Asctm. curvifolium* is used, plants are about half the size of a vanda. The dwarf species *Asctm. miniatum* gives very small-growing ascocendas that may be appropriate for home growing. Additionally, these types are also slightly less sensitive to cold.

However, many ascocendas are so highly bred with vandas that the ascocentrum influence is nearly lost,

resulting in large, cold-sensitive plants. Ascocentrums have a brilliant array of colors, ranging from blue and pink through reds, oranges, and yellows. Strong yellow ascocendas such as *Ascda.* Crownfox Honey Gold, *Ascda.* Freda Hartfield, *Ascda.* Fuchs Gold Button and *Ascda.* Crownfox Yellow Sapphire are relatively recent developments. Their fully saturated golden yellow color coupled with full rounded shape makes them the darlings of the judges wherever they are shown.

More typical of the miniature vanda-type ascocenda is *Ascda.* Motes Burning Sands, which, although it appears like a small *V. sanderiana*, is the result of crossing a yellowish ascocenda with the unusual *V. lamellata*. More like earlier ascocendas in shades of orange is *Ascda.* Candace's Sunshine. Exemplary of larger flowered, more vanda style ascocendas is *Ascda.* Joanne Jones, which is several generations removed from any ascocentrum influence, and so might not be as compact or adaptable as other smaller growing types.

**Below:** *Ascda.* Joanne Jones 'Crownfox' HCC/AOS. The very full form and dark wine color here shows the influence of generations of vanda breeding into ascocenda lines. Spring orchid shows provide an excellent opportunity to see the newest vandas and ascocendas in flower and for sale. Keep warm and humid and fertilize regularly.

**Right:** *Ascda.* Candace's Sunshine 'William Rogers' AM/AOS. Combining the famous breeder *Ascda.* Yip Sum Wah with *Asctm. miniatum* blood has resulted in this compact and brilliant flower. Modern varieties are much more uniform in flower quality and are easier to grow than in the past.

# CYMBIDIUMS

## SPRING CARE FOR CYMBIDIUMS

**Light:** Increasing light levels benefit these light-loving plants, making strong foliage and good flower stems.

**Water:** Water needs increase through this season because growth and flowers are both demanding of water resources.

**Fertilizer:** High nitrogen is a necessity to produce good growth early in season, which will allow best flower production later.

**Watch for:** Slugs and snails can be a problem for emerging flower stems. Repotting, if necessary, should be carried out by the end of this period, even at the expense of the long-lived flowers.

Cymbidiums have long been the harbinger of spring for West Coast orchid growers. Unfortunately, they are rather large and slow to bloom, which in concert with their need for cooler summer nights, makes them a poor choice for growers over most of the United States. Nevertheless, breeders continue to try to make cymbidiums with broader appeal. Whether having the look of a traditional pink cymbidium in a more compact plant, as in *Cym.* Grandiosa, or in more wildly diverging styles, such as the pendant *Cym.* Little Black Sambo and *Cym.* Next Generation, new types of cyms continue to be found that fascinate those who are able to grow them well. Indeed, pendant, or cascading, cymbidiums have been so popular in West Coast cymbidium circles that many seedlings are sold out before they even reach any appreciable size. Sometimes

they are sold to speculators who then charge exorbitant prices for these rarely seen plants.

The pendant types have the advantage of being best grown in hanging pots or baskets, so at least do not take up valuable bench space. The disadvantage is that they often have very coarse foliage. Many can be more difficult to grow, particularly those, such as *Cym.* Little Black Sambo, which are based on Australian hard-leaf species.

This type is intolerant of repotting at the wrong stage of the growth cycle and if a new growth is inadvertently broken the plant may simply languish and die.

The Australian types require more heat and higher light, making them better choices for Florida-like conditions and less appropriate for outdoors in southern California, where the cold and wet winters may spell death.

---

**Below left:** *Cym.* Little Black Sambo 'Mem. B.J. Curtis' FCC/AOS. Most are familiar with the traditional corsage-type rounded pastel cymbidiums but few are familiar with the pendant cyms with cascading flower stems. They are big plants, growing to more than 36" (91 cms) tall. They need a minimum of an 8" (20 cms) basket and require copious sun and water.

**Below:** *Cym.* Next Generation 'Everglades' AM/AOS – Combines two of the most popular species parents, *Cym. devonianum* as a grandparent and *Cym. madidum* as a parent. Best grown in a basket to allow display of the cascading spikes. Growers need to allocate plenty of room. Requires high light and warm temperatures.

# DENDROBIUMS

Dendrobiums, in all their myriad types, continue to be an important part of the spring flowering scene. While the often-seen hard cane types continue to be available during this season, it is other more unusual flowers that often draw the attention of growers. Indian dendrobiums, originating in the higher elevation, monsoon-oriented areas, have long been very popular for their floriferous habits. *Den. densiflorum* is just one of this group, which also includes *Den. aggregatum* and *Den. thrysiflorum*.

The key to success with this group is ample sunshine and water during the growing season, with an almost complete withdrawal of water and fertilizer, especially nitrogen, once the growths have matured in late summer and early fall. Otherwise, the plants simply will not flower.

Another dendrobium that requires this treatment is *Den. nobile,* the basis for an entire class of hybrids. Dendrobium species originating in the middle elevations of New Guinea have become increasingly popular over the past few years. They are notable for their often bizarre green-and-hairy blooms that can last for literally months on the plant. *Den. macrophyllum* is an excellent representative of this group. Plants require high light and ample warmth to do their best.

A firm favorite is *Den. amethystoglossum*, which grows very well as a basket subject in climates such as those found in south Florida. Finally, we are beginning to see more and more of the miniature cane types exemplified by *Den. unicum.* The brilliant orange flowers of this species, borne from nodes along the stem, are long-lasting additions to any spring display. *Den. unicum* is also proving to be a valuable parent in producing dwarf *Den. nobile* types for potted plant use.

A discussion of spring-flowering dendrobiums cannot pass without mention of the dendrobium relative, *Inobulbon munificum.* While this is not the easiest plant to grow, or even to buy, the unusual hairy bulbs and massive, branching sprays of flowers make this species well worth the effort of searching out and pampering.

**Left:** *Den. macrophyllum* is a member of the Latouria section of the genus from New Guinea. These moderately sized plants, which grow up to 15" (38 cms), require bright light and good warmth—60°Fahrenheit (16°Celsius) at night and 80°Fahrenheit (27°Celsius) during the day—to perform at their best. The long-lived blooms may appear in spring or fall. Like most dendrobiums, they prefer underpotting. Withholding fertilizer after the growth matures in the fall will often help to spur flowering.

**Right:** *Den. densiflorum* is a member of the Himalayan group of dendrobiums that includes *Den. thyrsiflorum*, *Den. lindleyi*, and *Den. farmeri*. *Den. densiflorum* is one of the tallest of the group, with plants reaching more than 18" (46 cms) when well grown. Best results are achieved with high light and warm temperatures—60°Fahrenheit (16°Celsius) nights and 80°Fahrenheit (27°Celsius) days—along with copious water and fertilizer during growth. When growth is ripe in the fall, begin to withhold water and eliminate all fertilizer to ensure spring bloom. Without an enforced rest, plants will not bloom. Available from specialist sources, this would be a good plant for those gardeners who can grow their plants outdoors during the summer.

# SLIPPER ORCHIDS

Spring is one of the peak seasons for slipper orchids, both paphiopedilums and phragmipediums. In paphs, almost all types are represented during the spring months. From the *Paph. insigne* based "Bulldog" types, such as *Paph.* Irish Lullaby and *Paph.* Silent Knight, to the Maudiae types, to the multifloras. One is liable to see just about any type of paph during the spring. *Paph.* Silent Knight illustrates the high plateau in this rare type reached by breeders over the past 15 years.

Such quality was only a dream, and seedlings are still rather closely held, hence expensive. *Paph.* Maudiae, first registered in 1900, is the archetype of an entire class of pot plant-type paphs, notable for their richly marbled foliage and easy-to-grow nature.

Today, we have a range of vibrant colors from red and wine colors, through mahogany and green. *Paph.* Rory Jones is just one example of the variation in color, yet uniformity in quality, in this breeding.

Another development from late in the last century was the vinicolor (wine colored) paphs based on a unique clone of *Paph. callosum.* Today, *Paph.* Cesar Delgado stands near the pinnacle of quality reached in this line of breeding. Indeed, plants that would have cost hundreds of dollars even 15 years ago are offered at $15 at your neighborhood garden center.

One of the most sought-after attributes of the "Maudiae" type paph is its extreme floriferousness, as seen in the beautifully grown plant of *Paph.* Petula. The degree to which shape has been improved over the relatively open flowers of the species can be seen in *Paph.* Mulyk's Macabre, with its very full shape and broad, heavily spotted petals.

A revolution in the production of multiflora paphs resulted from a vast proliferation of seed-raised species such as *Paph. rothschildianum* and *Paph. lowii.* Pictures showing a profusion of flowering *Paph. lowii* were unheard of until relatively recently. Beyond the great advances in flower and plant quality that this revolution has brought to the breeding pool, it has also meant that many previously unaffordable species are now available to the public at reasonable prices.

**Below:** *Paph.* Silent Knight 'Crystelle' AM/AOS. 'Bulldog,' or standard, paph come into their own in the spring. Plants are attractive even not in bloom with fans of broad dark green leaves. Keep evenly moist and shady, allowing plants to grow as large as possible before dividing.

**Right:** *Paph.* Petula 'Ann Krull' CCM/AOS. This Maudiae type orchid demonstrates why these are among the very best houseplant paphs. When allowed to grow large, alongside phals, they produce a display of handsome, long-lasting blooms. Keep evenly moist and do not overfertilize.

**Below:** *Paph. lowii.* This group of flowering seed-raised species slippers is one of the nicest of the strap-leaf types, requiring slightly more sun and more fertilizer than most paphs. The "flying" flowers are produced on tall stems of three to six 6" (15 cms) blooms.

This is yet another example of how responsible artificial propagation can reduce pressure on wild populations. Not only are more plants of the species available to hobby growers, but also their greater availability makes them more readily useful in further breeding.

Now we often see plants of such hybrids as *Paph*. Mcm. Rex van Delden, *Paph*. Lady Isabel, *Paph*. William Ambler, and *Paph*. Wild Thing offered where in the past they would have been closely held by the producer. We also see seed-raised populations of species like *Paph. moquettianum* and *Paph. micranthum*, species that until very recently would have come straight from their jungle habitat.

Not to be forgotten in any discussion of slippers are the New World slipper orchids, the phragmipediums. Whether in the exotic flame tones of *Phrag*. Sargeant Eric, the result of the newly discovered *Phrag. besseae*'s influence, or the subtle tones of the diminutive *Phrag. pearcei*, these plants have an appeal that transcends fashion. Many are proving to be faster growing than their Asian cousins, and others have a sequential blooming habit that extends their flowering season considerably. As an added bonus for those who cannot learn to water properly, it is almost impossible to overwater a phrag.

**Left:** *Paph. moquettianum.*
This and similar slippers
have the wonderful habit of
blooming sequentially, one
3" (8 cms) bloom opening as
the last fades, giving a display
that may last many months.
They prefer a shady and
humid situation and grow well
alongside phals. Do not be too
quick to divide, but when
plants are in need of potting
do not be afraid to sacrifice an
old flower spike because new
ones will follow.

**Right:** *Paph.* Lady Isabel
'Crystelle Smith' FCC/AOS.
Multiflora strap-leaf paphs
have reached a very high
plateau with the introduction
of improved forms of the once
rare species parents. Where
this type was once the domain
of the dedicated specialist,
more and more plants are
being raised for the open
market. Look for these at
spring orchid shows or at
specialty vendors.

**Right:** *Paph.* Mem. Rex van
Delden 'Danny Rodriquez'
AM/AOS. The brilliant golden-
yellow *Paph. armeniacum*
produces this distinctive and
highly awarded bloom. Best
results are attained with warm
temperatures and plenty of
moisture. This type is still
rather rare and hard to source,
although specialist nurseries
may be induced to part with
the occasional seedling.

# ONCIDIUMS

While the winter months are a low point for many of the various oncidium types—*Oncidium, Odontoglossum, Brassia, Miltonia*, and the many intergeneric hybrids—spring months begin to see an increasing number flower. Colombian miltonias or *Miltoniopsis*, those related to *Milt. vexillaria* and *Milt. roezlii*, begin to bloom in more profusion. Intergeneric hybrids also become more common, including the startling and exotic *Brassada* Orange Delight, a hybrid between the closely related genera of *Brassia* ('Spider Orchids') and *Ada*. This plant is particularly compact and floriferous owing to the characteristics of its *Ada* parent.

We also see the first of the more typical 'Dancing Lady' oncidiums, with their full-skirted yellow lips, including *Otoglossum scansor*, a species recently split off from *Oncidium*. Oncidium types begin to grow in earnest during spring months and new growths appear rapidly. Growers should pay close attention to potting needs to ensure that plants are potted at a favorable time. Oncidiums can quickly outgrow their pots, making potting and dividing more difficult, as well as damaging. Their robust root systems, which can easily fill a pot, suffer proportionately greater damage when overgrown because so much of the root mass has to be cut away to allow division.

**Right:** *Brassada* Orange Delight is made by crossing the dwarf *Brassia* relative *Ada aurantiaca* with a standard large spider orchid. Orange Delight is exemplary of the oncidium type plants that are becoming more widely available in the trade. Plants are often compact, growing to 15" (38 cms) or so. Per growth, they bear one or two stems of 6" (15 cms) long flowers in stunning orange tones. Keep evenly moist and moderately bright. These can be good houseplants in a bright window.

**Left:** *Otoglossum scansor.* Recently removed from its former home in the genus *Oncidium,* this curious orchid is for the discerning grower with a greenhouse. While its flowers are typical oncidium Dancing Lady, the plants are distinct. Small, rounded pseudobulbs give rise to long looping flower stems with widely spaced side branches with a few blooms each. New growths develop along the length of the flower spike. This plant is one that takes plenty of space and will grow rapidly.

# LYCASTE ORCHIDS AND THEIR RELATIVES

## SPRING CARE FOR LYCASTES

**Light:** None of these plants likes strong direct sun, so care should be given to guard against burning of the large broad leaves; bright, indirect light suits best.

**Water:** Water lightly as new growths emerge, stepping up frequency as leaves grow. Plants in full leaf can use copious amounts of moisture.

**Fertilizer:** Begin to increase fertilizer as watering frequency increases. Fertilizer should be appropriate to type of mix in use—generally high nitrogen with fir bark media.

**Watch for:** Potting needs; repot immediately after flowering. Over-wintering sucking pests will begin to appear on foliage. Foliage is very sensitive to oil-based sprays so care must be taken in application, which should be only during cool hours of morning or late afternoon.

Lycastes and their relatives—*Anguloa, Bifrenaria, Maxillaria* and others—put on their best show during the months of March, April, and May. Almost all of these genera tend to bloom from developing growths so as new growths come in the spring, so will flowers.

Anguloas, such as *Anguloa uniflora*, have robust pseudobulbs topped with broad, palm-like leaves. The multiple, single-flowered stems emerge from the base of the developing growth. These, like many lycastes and their intergeneric hybrid *Angulocaste*, are very large plants that are difficult to cultivate in the limited space available in the home. These are far better as patio plants in frost-free areas of the West Coast, in spacious greenhouses, or sunrooms. They are happy with cooler night conditions, around 50–60°Fahrenheit (10–16°Celsius), and make good sunroom subjects where nights are cool, but not cold.

Breeders have attempted to combine the colors and large size of the anguloas with lycastes, to mitigate the very cupped nature of the angula bloom. Over as little as one

**Left:** *Anguloa uniflora* are bold plants with large, up to 6" (15 cms) tall, pseudobulbs topped with broad, palm-like leaves that may reach 36" (91 cms) or more. The boat-shaped, heavy blooms are borne singly on tall stems. Requires lots of space and moderate temperatures, 60°Fahrenheit (16°Celsius) nights and 75°Fahrenheit (24°Celsius) days, along with high humidity and plenty of fresh, moving air.

**Above:** *Angst*. Santa Barbara 'Nike' AM/AOS. Lycaste breeding has progressed with fits and starts over the past 100 years. Hybridizers have added *Anguloa* to the mix in the attempt to broaden the color palette and to increase the substance. Angulocastes (*Anguloa* x *Lycaste*) are, like anguloas, large plants that require lots of room to do well. Keep evenly moist and humid.

generation, and extending into several, they have achieved great success, as in *Angst*. Olympus and *Angst*. Santa Barbara. The red of *Angst*. Santa Barbara is particularly rare and sought after. Additionally, many angulocaste hybrids tend to be winter deciduous so are leafless when in flower, allowing better viewing of the large and heavy-substanced blooms.

Traditional lycaste hybrids, those with heavy influence from the Guatemalan species *Lyc. skinneri*, are at their peak now. Hybrids such as *Lyc*. Koolena demonstrate the heights that this type has achieved, with extraordinarily full form and clear pink color. Red colors have also been introduced, after a long breeding process, to straight lycaste hybrids, as in the very fine *Lyc*. Always Kool. The

**Left:** *Max. tenuifolia.* The Coconut Pie Orchid, so-called for its enchanting fragrance, is a plant that almost anyone can grow. Exceptionally vigorous and free blooming, the 1" (2.5 cms) red blooms appear singly from the base of the growths. Basket culture is often the best choice for this species because it allows for longer periods between potting, which gives the plant a chance to grow into quite a specimen. Grow under intermediate conditions with moderate shade. Keep evenly moist and fertilize regularly.

**Right:** *Lyc.* Always Kool 'Crystelle' AM/AOS. *Lyc. skinneri* breeding reaches a pinnacle with plants like this. Large blooms, up to 6" (15 cms) or more, are borne singly from the base of robust pseudobulbs, usually in the spring. Available in shades of red, pink, and white from specialists, these plants are usually considered the domain of expert growers.

deciduous *Lycaste* species also put on a show in spring months, as with *Lyc. tricolor*.

*Maxillaria*, closely related to *Lycaste* and *Anguloa*, is another of the "super genera" owing to the many, many species in the genus—over 1,000 and counting. Perhaps no other genus has the diversity of plant habit and size, ranging from the miniscule *Max. ubatubana* to the enormous vining types rarely seen in cultivation. Rangy growth habit with rather long rhizomes between growths is the rule rather than the exception.

Probably the best known of the genus is *Max. tenuifolia*, the Coconut Pie Orchid, so-called for its wonderful fragrance. Smallish, blood-red blooms are borne singly from each growth and new growths are produced in such profusion that showy specimen plants are commonly seen. Unfortunately, there seem to be some cultivars that bloom more easily than others, so growers should be sure to look for old flower stems to ensure that they've gotten a bloomer.

Most maxillarias will thrive under shady intermediate conditions of 60°Fahrenheit (16°Celsius) nights and 75–80°Fahrenheit (24–27°Celsius) days. There are simply too many oddball species in this group to do more than picture a few, such as *Max. rufescens*, *Max. psuedoreichenheimina*, and *Max. rufescens*. As in any large genus, there are many rather plain and uninteresting flowers, but there are also some real jewels waiting for your discovery. *Bifrenaria* is another closely related genus, the best-known species being *Bif. harrisoniana*, a particular favorite of knowledgeable growers.

**Below:** *Max. rufescens.* Maxillaria is one of the largest—over 1,000 species—and most varied orchid genera. Frequently they have insignificant flowers, such as this cute species, and are unloved by many but treasured by the few. Grow under intermediate, shady conditions.

**Right:** *Bif. harrisoniae.* Bifrenaria is appreciated by experienced growers for its heavy substanced and fragrant blooms, offset by the hairy bluish lip. Plants are up to 15" (38 cms) tall with robust pseudobulbs. Flowers emerge in twos and threes from the base of the newest growth. Grow in intermediate conditions with 60°Fahrenheit (16°Celsius) nights and 80°Fahrenheit (27°Celsius) days and keep evenly moist.

Below: *Max. pseudoreichenheimiana.* This *Maxillaria* species has broad, medium-green leaves spotted with bold, silver blotches. The 3" (8 cms) yellow blooms are borne singly from the base of the newest growth. The plants are relatively compact and may make good indoor subjects for those who can grow their plants outdoors during summer months. Occasionally available from specialist growers, this one is worth a search.

# OTHER SPRING-FLOWERING ORCHIDS

While surveying the major groups of orchids that put on a show during spring, it is all too easy to overlook the less well-known players. The less obvious orchids can, however, add interest and variety to any collection. These range from the diminutive and easily accommodated members of the *Pleurothallid* group, such as *Pleurothallis* and *Masdevallia*, to the equally exotic

bulbophyllums, and range upward in size to the very large ansellias and sobralias, which are best left to those who have large patios or greenhouses.

Indoor or windowsill growers can choose from a variety of pleurothallis including *Pleur. nossax*, although not all are small, such as *Pleur. titan*. No other masdevallia is better known than *Masd. coccinea*. It is from higher elevations. Most of these plants require coolish temperatures and moist conditions.

Hailing from a similarly wide range of habitats are the Old World, bulbophyllums, which range from the tiny *Bulb. penicilloides* to the larger flower types such as *Bulb. sumatrana* and *Bulb. angustifolium*. Many bulbophyllums have long rhizomes and are not easily kept in a pot, so may do better mounted. However, high humidity and frequent watering is a necessity because they generally do not like to dry out between waterings. A wonderful home subject, more closely related to *Angraecum*, is *Sedirea japonica*, a miniature monopodial from Japan. Easily grown in a 3" (8 cms) or 4" (10 cms) pot, the attractive plant provides stems of leopard-spotted blooms that are highly perfumed. Grow this one with your phalaenopsis.

There is an astonishing selection of species and hybrids available to the grower with the space to house them. These larger, more demanding plants include members of such rarely seen genera as *Galeandra*, known for its tubular lips, and members of the catasetum group, most of which drop their leaves in winter to flower on bare, cigar-shaped pseudobulbs in the spring months. *Catasetum tenebrosum* is one of the finest and best known of this group and is highly prized for it extraordinarily dark blooms.

*Ansellia* is a genus originating in tropical Africa that is closely related to cymbidiums. Generally considered to have only one widely distributed and highly variable species, *Ans. africana* can range from compact, cattleya-size plants to a meter or more tall. Erect, branching inflorescences carry a multitude of variously spotted and barred mustard

**Left:** *Sedirea japonica* is a miniature orchid from Japan that is a perfect companion for the indoor phalaenopsis collection. Plants are no more than 3" (8 cms) tall and 12" (30 cms) across, with broad, flat leaves and arching stems of six to eight or more 1" (2.5 cms) fragrant blooms. Grow like a phal, keeping evenly moist and warm with nights around 60°Fahrenheit (16°Celsius) and days in the high 70s Fahrenheit (24–26°Celsius).

**Right:** *Masd. coccinea* 'Lois Posey' AM/AOS is a high elevation species that is not for everyone. While this is certainly one of the most beautiful of its genus, it will not thrive in areas where days go above 75°Fahrenheit (24°Celsius) and nights dip below 60°Fahrenheit (16°Celsius). The attractive leaves are 8" (20 cms) to 10" (25 cms) tall with flowers borne singly on stems to 15" (38 cms). Keep evenly moist with pure water for best results. Ample shade will help keep temperatures in check. Available from specialist nurseries.

Left: *Ansellia africana* 'Krull Smith' AM/AOS is a widespread species that has many forms, with plants that range from cattleya size to over 36" (91 cms). Best grown under cattleya conditions, where space is not an issue. Gardeners in frost-free areas often find this will succeed well on their patio. Allow to dry well between waterings and pot in media that allows infrequent potting.

Above: *Sobralia callosa*. Most sobralias are large plants, but this one is not, growing well in a 4" (10 cms) pot. The dwarf, bamboo-like foliage bears single blooms in succession from the apex of the cane. Intermediate conditions suit this plant well. Only occasionally available from specialist nurseries or importers.

yellow blooms, often offset by a nearly black lip. When in full bloom, one of the larger types from South Africa makes a rare sight. Some growers do not appreciate the musky fragrance. However, because these plants generally require so much space, they are often grown where the scent quickly dissipates. Cattleya conditions suit this genus well.

Finally, the Bamboo Orchid, *Sobralia*, begins to bloom in spring from the apex of the most recently matured canes. This is a widespread terrestrial New World genus that often

occurs en masse on open slopes or meadows. The flowers are borne in succession and last only a day or two. While most are larger plants, some few, such as *Sob. callosa*, are perfect miniature representations of their big brothers. Sobralias are not commonly seen, as few nurseries raise them from seed and imported plants do not reestablish easily because so much of their storage reservoir in their fleshy root is lost during transplanting.

# SUMMER-FLOWERING ORCHIDS

*With so much competition in the garden centers during the summers months, orchid breeders have shied away from summer bloomers. However, you can choose from a multitude of summer bloomers.*

## SUMMER CARE

### GENERAL

**Day length:** Longest, beginning to appreciably shorten near the end of the season; plants' growth rate at highest.

**Light:** Best quality of year, with sun at highest angle; highest proportion of sunny days; most likely season for deciduous trees to play a role in unfavorable light reduction for plants grown outside.

**Temperatures:** Warm days and nights; little or no danger of frost; best time of year for indoor plants to be outdoors.

**Overall:** Best time of year for almost all orchids; some caution during hottest months for high-elevation plants such as odontoglossums and masdevallias.

### GROWER RESPONSE

**Watering:** Often, at least once every seven days, depending on climate; some areas may see need for daily attention; tropical and subtropical areas see daily rains.

**Fertilizer:** Every watering at full strength; high nitrogen if desired; maximize growth opportunities.

**Watch for:** Heat-related problems; pest and disease problems can mushroom quickly in these favorable conditions; keep plants moist and well fertilized.

It may at first seem paradoxical that the season when orchids are visibly happiest, when they are growing most rapidly, is often when fewest orchids are naturally in flower. There are several reasons for this phenomenon.

First, both growing and flowering take a considerable amount of energy and it is seldom advantageous for both to go on simultaneously. That is not to say that it does not happen, but it is rather uncommon, especially in cultivated orchids. Even those that do flower in early summer make a rapid growth spurt in spring before putting up blooms.

Another reason may be that in most habitats, summer is when all plants are growing rapidly and there is simply too much competition for light and pollinators to make flowering an efficient use of energy. The intense competition in the native environs of many orchids is what first drove them into an epiphytic lifestyle. If the forest canopy is especially dense, it is more difficult for visually oriented pollinators to find the orchid flowers.

Also, there is greater competition from other forest species flowers, so orchid flowers, many of which rely on deception to attract pollinators—by resembling targets that give a nectar reward, when the orchid does not—are not attractive enough to overcome the other stimuli.

In a strictly horticultural sense, summer is a time of least interest for flowering orchid plants. There are simply too many other attractive alternatives in the garden that bloom only in summer, so orchids aren't likely to occupy much space in our busy schedules. This has had the result of growers, over the period of nearly 200 years, selecting plants for propagation that are not summer bloomers.

Today, though, as the market for flowering orchid

---

**Right:** *Epc.* El Hatillo. Two late spring flowering species, *Cattleya mossiae* and *Encyclia tampensis*, have combined to make this early summer-flowering variety. Compact plants, to only 8" (20 cms), branch freely to form large floriferous clumps, producing multiple stems of 2" (5 cms) green blooms. Very easy to grow with cattleyas or in the frost-free garden.

plants expands, demand for summer flowers is leading to the selection of summer-flowering orchids as well as the development of better seasonal control methods to force orchids into summer bloom.

## Maintenance

The sensible grower is busy with orchids during the summer months, doing all he or she can to enable the plants to take best advantage of the favorable growing conditions. This means potting when plants need it, watering thoroughly and regularly, fertilizing often, and keeping an eye out for potential problem areas so that they can be addressed before they become too serious.

These areas involve watching out for pests, diseases, too much sun or heat, occasional low humidity, or, conversely, overly high humidity over too long a period of time, which can lead to fungal and bacterial infections.

Plants that do flower during this period tend to develop their flowers or flower stems quite quickly. If not watched closely, the fast-growing stems can become caught under the foliage of other plants and deformed or be easily broken owing to the brittle nature of plant material produced under such rapid growth.

In areas of high summer rainfall, water should be kept off the flowers of outdoor orchids to avoid fungal spotting or physical damage. Indoor growing areas should be kept clean and well ventilated, both to provide the fresh, moving air that orchids require and to prevent the stratification of temperatures that may occur unless there is good mixing of air within the structure.

# VANDACEOUS ORCHIDS

Notable exceptions to the "rule" of not flowering while in active growth are the very tropical members of the vanda alliance. Because the plants do not grow except in times of high light, heat, and humidity and are nearly dormant during shorter day seasons, their flowering coincides with the warmer, growing-oriented months of June, July, and August. This is when the variety of shapes, sizes, colors, and forms in this group are at their best.

In more tropical areas, such as south Florida, this group is deservedly popular and makes up a significant portion of the "garden orchid" palette. Species like *Aerides houlletianum* and others in the genus make spectacular specimen plants in baskets or mounted in trees where their long flower stems give a breathtaking display. Ascocendas,

**Left:** *Ascda*. Crownfox Honey Gold 'Tangerine' HCC/AOS. Brilliant yellow ascocendas signal the beginning of summer. Copious water and warmth trigger the growing and flowering season for this type, which make outstanding patio subjects in subtropical areas such as south Florida. Grow in slatted wood baskets and fertilize regularly.

**Above:** *Aerides houlletianum* 'Mary Motes' HCC/AOS is a Southeast Asian species which forms large clumps of monopodial growths, ideal for baskets in subtropical gardens. The unusual 1" ( 2.5 cms) blooms are borne on densely packed foxtails and emit a lovely fragrance. Water freely during warm months and fertilize regularly.

**Left:** *Fcr.* Crownfox 'Sandy' AM/AOS. This new artificial genus is comprised of four genera, including the newly discovered *Christensoniana*. Relatively small plants, to 10" (25 cms), they produce semi-arching stems of 1" (2.5 cms) green blooms highlighted by a pink lip. Treat like other vandaceous orchids, though this might be suitable for indoor gardeners who can summer their plants outdoors, owing to its smaller size. Still rather rare, available occasionally from specialist nurseries.

**Right:** *V.* Alice Motes 'Daddy's Girl' AM/AOS is the result of continued breeding with species that have been underutilized. This vanda has a look all its own. It grows well with its cousins, though, and flowers freely throughout the year, with a peak in the summer.

such as *Ascda*. Crownfox Honey Gold and so many others, make stunning basket subjects, hanging in the patio or under trees.

The larger vandas, both species and hybrids, are also at their best during these warmest months. Traditional vandas with more *V. sanderiana* or *V. coerulea* influence, tend to bloom earlier in the year, while breeders have been extending the natural season of these plants by the use of less well-known species, achieving distinctive results like *V.* Alice Motes.

Southeast Asian orchid breeders have been particularly busy in creating a wide array of spectacular intergeneric hybrids within the *Vanda* group. These complex genera are rarely seen in the U.S. outside of south Florida, as they simply require too much heat and light to thrive in anything but perfect conditions.

However, we do see some of the best of this group brought in by Florida nurseries, and they are generally very careful to introduce subjects that will succeed under a wider variety of conditions. Unfortunately, not many of these are satisfactory home or underlights subjects and are best limited to the greenhouse or subtropical and frost-free garden.

There are a few examples that have been bred from more tolerant and smaller-growing species, and these hybrids can find wider applicability. One such new hybrid group is *Fuchsara*, a complex intergeneric collection of plants containing *Vanda*, *Ascocentrum*, *Rhyncostylis*, and the relatively newly discovered *Christensoniana*. The Vietnamese species *Christensoniana* lends the hybrid *Fcr.* Crownfox its green color and nice, upright spike on a very compact plant.

# CATTLEYAS

Cattleyas are becoming a more and more important group for summer flowering. South American growers are responding to demand by the introduction of the finest examples of their summer flowering species, and hybrids with a summer bloom habit are rating more highly in the plans of domestic nurserymen.

Cattleyas are certainly beautiful and easy to grow, but their wide range of seasons is what gives them an edge when it comes to quickly filling in seasonal gaps.

Unifoliate, large-flowered species of cattleyas are fairly common and bloom from a growth developed during the late spring and early summer. The sheath forms with the new growth, and bud formation occurs almost immediately as the growth firms up. This is in contrast to spring bloomers in this group, which flower from a lead growth

**Left:** *C. gaskelliana.* Summer-blooming cattleyas produce their flowering stems from the most recently developed pseudobulb before the growth is completely ripe. Potting is best left until immediately after flowering when new roots emerge from the base of the growth. A variety of color forms are available.

**Above:** *C. warneri semi-alba* blooms after *C. gaskelliana,* in July. Latin-American nurseries have introduced several new forms in recent years, including this beautiful semi-alba (white with colored lip), example. *C. warneri* tends to have stockier, shorter plants than *C. gaskelliana,* to 10" (25 cms) or so.

or growths made up the preceding season. Because these species, *C. warneri, C. warscewiczii* (aka *C. gigas*), *C. gaskelliana,* and *C. dowiana,* bloom from soft growth, growers may sometimes have trouble discerning when to repot. If in doubt, immediately after flowering is always a good time to pot cattleyas that bloom in the late spring. *C. warneri* and *C. gaskelliana* are not dissimilar members of the group, with large, light lavender blooms that begin to show as early as June for *C. gaskelliana* and into July with *C. warneri.*

As with most unifoliate cattleyas, a variety of color forms beyond the typical lavender types are often seen, including, most commonly, blue—known as coerulea, semi-alba and white. *C. warscewiczii*, as its former name *C. gigas* might indicate, is one of the largest growing and flowered of the unifoliates, with plants often over 30 inches (76 cms) tall, and flowers to 9 inches (23 cms). This is one of the most imposing of all cattleya species and has been very important in the development of modern hybrids.

**Below:** *C. warscewiczii*, was once known as *C. gigas*. Both the plant and the flower are among the very largest in the genus and make an impressive display. Plants may reach up to 30" (76 cms) in height. *C. warscewiczii* follows *C. warneri*, blooming from later July into August.

**Right:** *C. dowiana* is probably the most difficult of the cattleyas to grow. The plants are particularly sensitive to potting at the wrong time. Well-grown plants will give three or four 6" (15 cms) blooms with a wonderful fragrance.

**Left:** *C. leopoldii* is a bifoliate species which makes a good showing in summer months. *C. leopoldii* is one of the largest bifoliate cattleyas, reaching 48" (122 cms) or more on mature plants. Clusters of up to a dozen or more waxy, spotted blooms may last weeks in perfection. Pot only when new roots emerge.

**Above:** *Lc.* Amphion 'Mem. Frieda Duckitt' AM/AOS. This remake of an antique hybrid, using a superior form of the *L. tenebrosa* parent, shows all the charm of the species. It grows much like its parents and demands attention be paid to potting times. Plants are tall, to 24" (61 cms), with 6" (15 cms) blooms.

Happily, these species are being reintroduced as seed-raised plants by both offshore and domestic growers, and are proving to be much easier to grow than the wild-collected plants of years past. *C. dowiana*, and the closely related *C. aurea*, from Costa Rica and Colombia, are yellow-flowered unifoliate cattleyas. These species are some of the most important sources of not only yellow coloration in modern hybrids but also the best semi-albas and darkest purples, which also owe a great deal to *C. dowiana* ancestry. Unfortunately, *C. dowiana* is notorious as one of the most difficult of all cattleyas to consistently grow well.

Consistency is key as *C. dowiana* is more prone to a quick death as a result of a cultural mistake than any other cattleya. However, when the culture is correct—which involves more warmth than is typical and great care is given in potting season—the flowers, with their rich, yellow color and striking, red and gold-veined lips, and sweet perfume, are among the most rewarding of all orchids. There are also exciting summer flowering unifoliate hybrids based in *C. dowiana* and *L. tenebrosa*, such as the very showy *Lc. Amphion*.

Summer is when the bifoliate cattleyas—those species and their derived hybrids with more than two leaves per

**Above left and right:** *C. schofeldiana* is one of the seldom seen, smaller members of the genus, growing to only 20" (51 cms). It is bifoliate, with several 5" (13 cms) olive-colored blooms with fine red spotting. Care should be taken to pot only when needed and when appropriate. A plant for the grower who must have every form of cattleya.

growth—really come into their own. Highly seasonal in their growth cycle, new leads initiate as days lengthen and warm. The growths reach their mature size in the few months of summer to flower at the appropriate time, which is often late summer. The first to flower are the rose lavender *C. harrisoniana* and *C. loddigesii* types, along

with the closely related *C. intermedia*, followed closely by the bronze heads of *C. leopoldii* and the rare *C. leopoldii alba*. While bifoliate cattleya blooms tend to be a bit smaller, they more than compensate for their size with rich colors and many more flowers per stem, occasionally as many as 15 or more. *C. harrisoniana* and *C. loddigesii* are more compact than the majestic *C. leopoldii*, usually about 18 inches (45 cms) tall, while *C. leopoldii* and the slightly later blooming *C. guttata* reach upwards of 48 inches (123 cms) or more. Primary hybrids in this group are among the showiest orchids for summer with *C. resplendens* (*schilleriana* × *guttata*) leading the way.

*C. schofeldiana* blooms somewhat later in summer, with more muted tones of bronzy green offset by a rose-veined white lip. Some forms may have pronounced spotting or more bronze cast to the coloration. This species is not so commonly seen and is worth searching out to complete a collection of cattleya species. *C. bicolor*, along with *C. guttata*, is the tallest growing cattleya, flowering during August. A rose lip, often outlined in white, highlights the green blooms. *C. bicolor* has a fairly wide range in Brazil and several color forms may be seen, including those that have more bronze or deeper green color. A smaller-growing bifoliate primary hybrid that shows off in the late summer

is C. Quinquecolor, nicely intermediate between its two parents, C. *aclandiae* and C. *forbesii*.

There are a wealth of summer blooming cattleya hybrids, both bifoliate and otherwise. The bifoliate species are popularly used with more complex hybrids to create very saturated colors as in *Lc*. Summerland Girl, an older C. *guttata* hybrid that retains its beauty and value when stacked against newer varieties. The bifoliates have also been useful in the production of sought-after green hybrids. The alba (pure green with a white lip) form of C. *leopoldii* has been very influential in green hybrids, as have other green bifoliates, with such progeny such as *Blc*. Hawaiian Passion leading the way in modern greens. Breeders have gone down some interesting byways with bifoliates in an effort to create spotted flowers, one of the more recently developed being C. Pink Leopard, a combination of several species. Spotted breeding takes an unexpected turn when

**Above:** *Lc*. Summerland Girl has earned a place in the ranks of classic cattleyas. Rich red color and waxy substance set the 4" (10 cms) flowers apart. Plants are moderately sized 24" (61 cms) in bloom. The stems bear four to a dozen well-held blooms in mid-summer.

**Right:** C. Quinquecolor. Two bifoliate species, C. *aclandiae* and C. *forbesii*, combine to produce this distinctive plant. They are very compact, to only 8" (20 cms), making them suitable for indoor growers who are able to summer their plants outdoors.

C. *aclandiae* is introduced in the second generation, here illustrated by *Slc*. Leopard Lou, a miniature spotted flower. Another unusual result from bifoliate breeding is the combination of the splash petal form of C. *intermedia* (known as Aquinii) with the late spring blooming *L. purpurata* to make *Lc*. Schilleriana. This sort of hybrid also finds favor among cymbidium enthusiasts.

**Above left:** *Slc.* Leopard Lou 'KG's Redwing' AM/AOS. Modern "minicatt breeding" produces some of the most flamboyant color combinations seen in cattleyas. A mix of *C. aclandiae*, *C. guttata*, *C. intermedia*, and *Soph. coccinea* results in plants that remain dwarf, to less than 8" (20 cms), with three or four gaudy blooms.

**Left:** *C.* Pink Leopard. Its parents are *C.* Penny Kuroda and *C.* Lulu, itself a hybrid that is one-half *C.* Penny Kuroda. Boldly spotted over a pearly background, *C.* Pink Leopard is slightly larger growing, to 12–15" (30–38 cms), and has up to six or more 4" (10 cms) blooms.

**Above:** *Blc.* Hawaiian Passion. *Blc.* Waikiki Gold, one of the parents here, has proven to be an exceptional breeder for greens and yellows, often with an enchanting fragrance. Plants remain compact, to 15" (28 cms), with a cluster of four to six 4" (10 cms) blooms that are very long lasting. Good for indoors or with other cattleyas, these types are often available from Hawaiian nurseries and seen at spring orchid shows.

# BRASSAVOLA ORCHIDS

Another of the distinctive cattleya-alliance genera that put on a display during summer months are the brassavolas and their hybrids. Brassavolas are notable for their often bizarrely shaped blooms of greenish white, which are heavily perfumed at night to attract night-flying pollinators, such as moths. *B. cucullata* and its hybrid *B.* David Sander illustrate the genus well but are less commonly seen than the better known Lady of the Night, *B. nodosa*. This orchid is often cited as one of the best beginners plants, and as one of the most satisfactory of all orchids. It is easy to see why. The plants are compact, with quill-like leaves that may be upright or pendant. Pot, basket, or mount culture all work for this species, and when it gives its wealth of serenely beautiful blooms, the entire area is filled with a lovely fragrance in the night hours. One could do far worse than a basket of this orchid on the terrace outside when planning a romantic evening. Add all these fine traits in with ease of culture and an intrinsic value as a parent and it is hard to surpass *B. nodosa* as an orchid worth searching out.

**Left:** *Brassavola* David Sander. This is a hybrid between the two types of *Brassavola*—the true *Brassavola* species *B. cucullata* and *Rhyncolaelia digbyana*. Has 8" (20 cms) flowers with a wonderful night fragrance. A tolerant plant that grows like other cattleyas; it needs bright light and to dry between waterings.

**Above:** *B. nodosa* or the Lady of the Night orchid is an all-timer, one no collection should be without. *B. nodosa* is a willing subject, surviving neglect and rewarding care. The ghostly blooms may be borne several times throughout the year under good conditions, with a flowering peak in summer.

# CATTLEYA RELATIVES

Encyclias are also at their best during summer months. The genus is full of easy-to-grow and floriferous species, many of which have gone on to be of value as parents, as well. *Enc. plicata* and *prismatocarpa* are just two representatives of this genus worth growing. *Enc.* Orchid Jungle, a primary hybrid, is a very famous plant with a multitude of showy cultivars. *Epicat* El Hatillo, a hybrid of the Florida native *Enc. tampense* crossed with *C. mossiae*, is a very cute and floriferous orchid for pot culture, quickly making a multispiked specimen plant in a relatively small pot. There is also a good selection of Brazilian laelias to be had for summer bloom. Two extremes in size in this diverse group, both with yellow blooms, are the diminutive *L. briegerii* and the larger *L. xanthina*, a relative of *L. purpurata*. *L. briegerii* is one of the rupicolous or rock-dwelling laelias, and is not always easy to grow well. Small pots of inert mix will enable the grower to best control watering.

**Left:** *Laelia briegerii* is a native of Brazil which requires bright, diffused light. In the summer months, it needs frequent watering, but roots must be dried rapidly after watering. Apply half-strength fertilizer high in nitrogen on a weekly basis when the plants are growing vigorously in the summer.

**Above:** *Enc.* Orchid Jungle 'Tom's Heritage' AM/AOS. This primary hybrid has been remade, selfed (crossed with itself) and sibling crossed (two different siblings crossed together) many times. Plants become large, to 24" (61 cms) or more, over time and produce long, branching stems of colorful 2" (5 cms) blooms.

# PHALAENOPSIS

## SUMMER CARE FOR PHALAENOPSIS

**Light:** Guard against burning as light intensity is at its highest, and soft foliage is susceptible to damage. Strong light, however, will give the best flower production.

**Water:** Keep potting medium moist at all times; watering may be required every three to four days in bright, warm, and well-ventilated situations.

**Fertilizer:** Feed regularly with full-strength fertilizer alongside increased watering.

**Watch for:** Sun burn and pests that can multiply quickly under warm conditions on fast-growing plants. It is potting time for all plants not finished flowering during spring. Cut spikes if necessary so as not to miss the best growing season.

Two popular groups that are not well represented in the summer are the slippers and phalaenopsis. Summer flowering phalaenopsis are limited to those few that naturally flower in this season, such as *Phal. lueddemanniana* and the closely related *Doritis* species and their hybrids. The phals that flower in summer are, by and large, less often seen in popular cultivation because they tend to have fewer flowers in more unusual tones. That is not to say that phals are not available in summer, because commercial growers often control flowering to enable them

Below: *Phal. lueddemanniana.* Summer months see a decline in the number of phals available, with the novelty types generally predominating. Species like *Phal. lueddemanniana* help fill the gap with shiny green plants and unusual, barred blooms. The 2" (5 cms) blooms are borne a few at a time on long, looping stems.

to produce during other months. There are, of course, always those stragglers that remain in bloom from their spring season, and the flower spikes may have to be sacrificed on these to enable the grower to get his potting done in a timely fashion. Some growers find themselves drawn to the more unusual species in flower at this time, such as *Phal. violacea* and similar types.

**Below:** *Phal.* Joy Spring Canary. Brilliant yellow flowers of this quality were once unobtainable except by the very wealthy. Today, your local garden center may be the source you are looking for. Plants generally bear fewer flowers—to eight or so—than standard types. Grow alongside the rest of your phals and pot when new roots emerge. This color range may tend to be more cold sensitive, so keep night temperatures on the warm side.

# SLIPPER ORCHIDS

## SUMMER CARE FOR SLIPPER ORCHIDS

**Light:** Strong summer light conditions will need muting for the best growth of plants. Use additional shading as necessary to keep light and heat levels reasonable.

**Water:** Relatively quick growth means frequent watering is needed to maintain even moisture in the pot.

**Fertilizer:** Highest rates of the year are allowable now, though paphs are always better with less food than more, so never use full-strength. Try a lower dose.

**Watch for:** Sunburn and pests, which can multiply quickly under warm conditions on fast-growing plants. It's potting time for all plants not finished up during spring.

Paphiopedilums, like phalaenopsis orchids, are not often seen flowering in summer months. The exceptions to the rule are the Maudiae types, as seen in *Paph*. Bob Nagel, a fine albino green and a useful addition to any houseplant collection. Both parents of *Paph*. Maudiae, *Paph. callosum* and *Paph. lawrenceanum*, are orchids that flower during summer months, as well. However, the real show that well-grown paphs put on in the summer is most often their multitoned foliage. Many of our most popular paphs have finely marked, marbled, and otherwise tessellated foliage that looks at its best during the summertime, as the plants grow rapidly in preparation for the flowering season to come.

**Left:** *Paph*. Mulyk's Macabre 'Krull Smith' AM/AOS. High quality Maudiae types can now be found at local garden centers. Ideal houseplant companions to phalaenopsis, the long-lasting 4" (10 cms) blooms are borne on tall stems above marbled foliage. It's time to repot when the medium breaks down; this can be done at almost any season. Keep evenly moist and do not overfertilize.

**Above:** *Paph*. Bob Nagel 'New Horizon' AM/AOS. This tetraploid slipper demonstrates the heights to which modern Maudiae types have risen. The plant's full form and broad petals mark this as a winner. As with the red and coloratum types, the alba greens make wonderful houseplants and are widely available from a variety of sources.

# DENDROBIUMS

Two of the earliest dendrobium-related species to flower are *Epigeneium lyonii* and *Dockrillia wasselii*. *E. lyonii* is very showy but rarely seen in collections. However, enterprising nurserymen are beginning to propagate this, and other unusual species from seed, leading to increased ease of availability. However, it is a slow-growing orchid so should only be attempted by patient gardeners. *Dockrillia wasselii*, from Australia,

---

**Right:** *Epigeneium lyonii* produce one or two, often-branching inflorescences. The flower stems are strong and upright, as well as about one-half the height of typical hybrid phalaenopsis, growing to 18" (46 cms) and bearing eight to twelve or more 3" (8 cms) blooms.

---

**Far right:** *Dockrillia wasselii* originates in Australia and has only recently been separated from *Dendrobium*. Plants make a fine specimen of small, upright, quill-like succulent leaves that quickly fill a slatted basket.

**Left and right:** *Den. goldschmidtianum,* aka *Den. miyakei* can grow to 3 feet (91 cms) high and 4 feet (122 cms) across. The clusters of rose-striped flowers are borne on second-year canes. Semishade and cattleya conditions suit this one best. Larger plants will produce flowers throughout the year. Basket culture suits this type well, allowing plants to achieve a large size without having to repot overmuch.

makes a fine specimen plant of small, upright, quill-like succulent leaves that quickly fill the pot or slatted basket. In early summer, after a pronounced dry rest, heads of spidery white blooms rise above the plants like clouds. This one does well located with cattleyas.

*Den. goldschmidtianum,* aka *Den. miyakei,* is one of the nicest of the smaller-growing species, with clusters of long-lived, rose-striped flowers produced on second-year canes. Semishade and conditions that favor cattleyas suit this orchid best. Because it flowers on older, leafless canes, be

sure never to remove old growths until you are sure that they have finished flowering. Larger plants will "flush" with flowers throughout the year.

Finally, one of the more interesting dendrobiums to bloom at this season is the rarely seen, though increasingly popular, *Den. hainanensis.* Plants appear almost grass- or bamboo-like, with the medium-size, brilliant yellow blooms interspersed throughout from random leaf nodes. The appearance is not unlike the surprise appearance of a buttercup in a field of grass.

# ONCIDIUM TYPES

## SUMMER CARE FOR ONCIDIUM TYPES

**Light:** Watch for burning in strong light conditions; some additional shade may be necessary to protect the broad, soft leaves.

**Water:** Water needs will be high during active growth, with vigorous root growth quickly filling pots.

**Fertilizer:** Full strength with a formula that is appropriate to the medium used.

**Watch for:** Spider mites in dry conditions. Keep leaves clean, top and bottom, by frequent syringing with water.

Oncidium types begin to be seen toward the end of summer, as growths mature, but there are a few, such as *Rossioglossum* (aka *Odontoglossum*) *williamsonianum* that bloom from new growths and are seen during the summer. Also in this species are such old favorites as *Ross. grande*, the Tiger Orchid. Unfortunately, these are not easy

**Below:** *Rossioglossum williamsianum.* This desirable species has become difficult to find. Distinctive plants with broad, matte gray-green leaves, to 15" (38 cms), produce tall stems of 6" (15 cms) "tiger" blooms in summer from new growths. Grows with cattleyas or cymbidiums, give a dry rest during winter months.

for growers to propagate from seed, and wild-collected plants are not easily available. However, both species are worth the search. Both will also grow under garden conditions in frost-free, cymbidium-friendly climates. Brazilian, or "true," miltonias also begin to bloom in late summer from growths made up in spring and early summer. Most of this genus are rather rampant in their growth, with substantial distance between bulbs, so are best accommodated on slabs or in baskets. Best known of this group is *Milt. spectabilis*, in both its typical rose pink form and grape-purple Moreliana variety. This is one of the easiest of all orchids to grow under conditions that favor either cattleyas or cymbidiums.

---

**Below:** *Miltonia spectabilis* makes an excellent mount or basket subject and is very prolific. Grows with cattleyas or cymbidiums, making a good garden plant in frost-free areas. Allow to dry between waterings and position in bright light.

# "SOFT LEAF" ORCHIDS

Orchid aficionados have labeled one of the least known, but most attractive, group of orchids the "soft leaf" group. Related to zygopetalums, genera like *Bollea*, *Huntleya*, and *Chondrorhynca* have growths comprised of a fan of soft, medium green leaves with no visible pseudobulbs. A nicely-grown plant of one of these genera is simply pretty. The single blooms emerge from the leaf axils on short stems, and the plant will often have to be elevated for the flowers to be seen easily. Two of the larger growing species in this group are *Huntleya meleagris* and *Huntleya wallisii*, with fans that may reach 18" (45 cms). Huntleyas may also produce longer rhizomes between growths than many in this group, resulting in plants that appear to "climb" out of the pot. Nevertheless, the year-round decorative quality of the plants, coupled with the waxy and unusual blooms, make these plants worth searching out and pampering.

Shady and moderate conditions suit this group best, with smallish pots to house the large root systems and an allowance for more frequent watering. The closely related *Galeottia fimbriata* flowers a bit later, in August, but will enjoy similar conditions. Its blooms are highly distinctive and long lasting. Because this group of plants generally inhabits lower levels in the forest, where moisture is more constant, they are intolerant of poor-quality water, which can lead to stunted root systems and burnt leaf tips. Growers in poor quality water areas, such as the arid Southwest or southern California, will achieve best results by keeping the plants quite moist and never allowing them to dry completely because this will help avoid over-concentration of the soil solution and its attendant problems.

**Left:** *Huntleya meleagris*. Huntleyas are part of the *Zygopetalum* group. Plants have no pseudobulbs and form large, to 15" (38 cms) or more, fans of broad leaves, giving an attractive appearance. The waxy, 4" (10 cms) blooms are produced singly from the leaf axils. Best results are attained when the plants are underpotted.

ove: *Bollea coelestis* 'David Manzur' FCC/AOS. A truly stunning
mple of this extraordinary Colombian species. One of the "soft leaf"
es related to *Zygopetalum*, the fan-shaped plants are attractive even
en not in bloom. Grow cool and somewhat shady, in proportionately
ll pots.

# SOBRALIAS

Gardens with larger growing areas or those in frost-free areas that allow outdoor growing, can enjoy sobralias during summer months. Sobralias grow rapidly with the onset of longer summer days, creating the bamboo-like canes that will flower in the following year. This genus is known for its exceptionally robust root system, which also serves as a water and nutrient reservoir during dry months.

Sobralias are just now beginning to become better known to gardeners and more are being introduced each year. While many resemble typical lavender cattleyas, some are pristine white, as are *Sob. virginalis* and *Sob. fragrans*. While the flowers may last only a day or so, they open in succession over a period of weeks, giving a long-lasting and beautiful display. Sobralias need plenty of water and fertilizer during summer months and are among the orchids requiring highest light levels.

**Right:** *Sob. virginalis* comes from higher elevations and hence does well alongside cymbidiums, where the bamboo-like plants make a nice foliar contrast. Large, to 6" (15 cms), white, cattleya-like blooms are borne successively during summer months. Keep evenly moist and fertilize regularly. Pot infrequently in a terrestrial mix, making sure not to injure the husky roots because they provide much-needed nutrient storage.

**Below:** *Sob. decora* is a low-elevation plant of the New World tropics and does best as a garden plant in warmer areas owing to its large size. Bamboo-like canes grow to 30" (76 cms) and bear blooms successively, one 4" (10 cms) flower at a time, over a period of months during the summer. Keep evenly moist and fertilize regularly. This plant is rarely available and only then from specialist nurseries.

# OTHER SUMMER-FLOWERING ORCHIDS

While some of the *Catasetum/Cycnoches* group flower in the winter and spring from deciduous pseudobulbs, others flower from newly produced summer growths. Because of the *Galeandra* parent, the unusual intergeneric hybrid *Catasandra* Fanfare flowers during summer and retains its leaves during flowering. *Clowesia russeliana* is admired for its pendant stems of green bells, while the popular *Catasetum pileatum*, the Swan Orchid, may have either large male blooms, which are most usually seen, or smaller, more bizarre, female blooms.

Unisexual flowers, those with either male or female parts, are more often seen in this group of genera than in

**Below:** *Catasetum pileatum* 'Lunar Dream'. Catasetums are deciduous orchids that can produce either male or female flowers. Here we see the male bloom. The cigar-shaped growths have broad leaves. Grow bright and warm, giving copious water when growing, withholding water after growth is mature.

**Right:** *Clowesia russeliana* is closely related to *Catasetum*, but produces bisexual blooms with plants that are slightly smaller, to around 18" (46 cms) or so. Both groups broad, soft leaves are subject to spider mite infestation in warm and dry conditions, so maintaining humidity is a must.

**Left:** *Dendrochilum magnum* is the "magnum" sized member of this otherwise diminutive genus. Plants may reach nearly 20" (51 cms). The flowers produce a spectacular chain-like display and have a characteristic musky fragrance. Grow with cattleyas on the shady side.

**Right:** *Lockhartia oerstedii*. Lockhartias are infrequently seen but are prized by cognoscenti for their "braided" plants. The growths feature overlapping, bract-like leaves with flushes of oncidium-like yellow blooms throughout the year. Grow in baskets or on mounts to display the beautiful plants. Best placed with cattleyas, slightly shady.

others. The sex of the flowers is influenced by heat and light. Growers need to take care with this group during warm summer months because spider mites can rapidly build up on the broad, soft foliage, causing great damage. Maintenance of good humidity levels and frequent syringing (washing) of the undersides of the leaves will help keep these pests under control.

Finally, there are the "one-offs" that don't fit into any category. *Ida fragrans*, formerly placed in *Lycaste*, blooms in August with a flush of creamy green nodding blooms. Despite the name change, this species will grow quite happily with its former brethren under shady conditions.

*Coelogyne pandurata* is one that has been known as a black orchid, owing to the strong black markings on its lip. Otherwise the flower is a fetching apple green. This is a large plant, suitable only for greenhouse culture in warmer climates where it does best in baskets. The rhizomes between bulbs are 4–6 inches (10–15 cms) long, leading to a plant that quickly escapes from whatever pot attempts to contain it. Some find that slabs work well for this showy species. Short-lived, but extraordinarily showy and fragrant, stanhopeas are not for everyone. The descending flower stems demand basket culture. *Stanhopea grandiflora* is unusual in this genus for its nodding white blooms. Despite the short flower life, specialist growers seek these out for the excitement of the exotic blooms.

Not all orchids are grown for their individual blooms. Some are treasured for the display given by their flowering stem as a whole. Both notylias and dendrochilums have flowers that, taken singly, are rather nondescript. However, taken as a whole, the inflorescences give a display that is very decorative and pleasing. *Dendrochilum magnum*, as the name implies, is the largest of the genus and has a musky fragrance. *Notylia barkeri* is also very decorative, with fringed green blooms in profusion on quite compact plants. And some orchids are valued simply for their unusual growth habit. Lockhartias, the Chain orchid, are grown as much for the striking appearance of their overlapping leaves as for the oncidium-like yellow blooms. *Lockhartia oerstedii* is one of the better known of this uncommon genus. A full pot of this orchid provides year-round interest.

# FALL-FLOWERING ORCHIDS

*With the extremes of summer heat passed, the oncidium varieties come to the fore—and as light levels dip, both watering and fertilizer levels can be reduced.*

## FALL CARE

### GENERAL

**Day length:** Shortens as the sun's angle in the sky decreases. Plants growth begins to slow in preparation for winter.

**Light:** Quality is still good. Keep light levels high to mature developing growth and encourage flowering.

**Temperatures:** Can still be some of the warmest in the year. Nights may begin to cool toward the end of the period in more northerly areas. Frost remains rare but can be a factor.

### GROWER RESPONSE

**Overall:** Still plenty of good growing time remaining. Maximize growth with water and fertilizer. Prepare for cooler months by beginning to clean up plants so that they're ready for moving indoors.

**Watering:** Still summer frequency, lessening to once a week nearer end of period; can be a very dry time of year, requiring close monitoring of atmospheric moisture.

**Fertilizer:** Full strength at beginning, reducing to half strength near the end of the period; low nitrogen fertilizer may be indicated for winter dormant types.

**Watch for:** Dryness and pests, which can quickly buildup on summer growth. Begin to prepare for winter and look for first signs of budding from winter bloomers.

The transitional nature of fall as a season is much more pronounced and demanding of grower attention than spring. The positive effects of increased light and day length appear in spring without any significant grower intervention, while in the fall months, observant gardeners must watch for changing conditions quite diligently and react appropriately.

Additional shading, necessary during bright summer months, can be removed to take maximum advantage of still bright days. Plants require less frequent watering and begin to respond to shortening days and the lowering sun angle by completing the growth they began during the spring and summer.

Ripening growths require less nitrogen and a low nitrogen fertilizer may be indicated, particularly for dendrobiums and cymbidiums. Nights cool and heating arrangements—unneeded during summer—must be checked, with any deferred maintenance performed before the first frosty days. Plants that have been summered outdoors have to be prepared for their transition to indoor facilities. This means a general cleanup and inspection. Look for potential pest problems that should be solved before bringing plants indoors where pests will have the chance to build up over the winter.

Greenhouses should be checked for any holes or breakage in the covering that might allow heat to escape during cold months. Potting should have already been completed, but there will be the odd plant here and there that may simply need it before next spring. Take advantage of what little growing time there is left to attempt to get this type of plant established before winter.

**Right:** *Trigonidium egertonianum.* Widespread in Central and northern South America, this warm-growing species would be a good companion for phalaenopsis under slightly shady conditions in the home. Plants comprise closely set pseudobulbs, grassy upright leaves, and single flowers. Keep moist and in slightly undersize pots.

Plants that require an enforced winter rest will need to be gradually weaned from watering, until, by the end of November or so, they are kept completely dry until growth begins again. There are a whole list of chores that the savvy grower will want to complete before winter, with its cold temperatures and short days, sets in. Above all, fall is the time to enjoy the fruits of the summer's growth, and there is no better way to do this than spending time with your plants. The best growers know to enjoy the plants performance and appearance first, in the sure knowledge that well-grown plants will give them maximum floral display.

# ONCIDIUM TYPES

For so many reasons, potted phalaenopsis are by far the world leader in terms of sales. However, commercial orchid growers, ever on the lookout for "the next big thing," have long debated what could or would rival the marketplace success of phals. Today, it seems that the extraordinary diversity of the *Oncidium* group makes it the logical choice. And it is in the fall months that we see the greatest variety of *Oncidium* species and hybrids.

Of course, oncidiums are available year round in fairly good supply, or they could not be the success that they are. However, many growers find that they have a distinct peak in the fall months after a good summer's growth. The sheer range of colors and patterns, the floriferous nature of the plants, and the showers of blooms that even a modest plant may produce all add up to one of the most satisfactory of all orchid groups.

Because members of this group of genera—including *Oncidium, Odontoglossum, Brassia, Miltonia, Miltoniopsis, Comparettia, Cochlioda*—are so wide-ranging in habitat, it is difficult to make too many generalizations about their care. However, and as with the similarly large genus *Dendrobium*, this group does best if not overpotted.

It is tempting, given the often lush top growth that these plants will produce, to calculate the size of pot for the top of the plant rather than the root mass. Indeed, many beginners, noting the vigorous root growth in a small pot and believing that "bigger is better," overpot, thinking that the roots will also fill the larger pot. In most cases, they will not, and the net effect will be a smaller root mass that is less able to support the plant well.

If a plant is underpotted and quickly fills its pot with roots, it is, while requiring more frequent watering, actually better able to support the top of the plant because the healthy root system will not only take up but also store water much more efficiently and thoroughly. Beyond this generalization, it becomes counterproductive to give too

**Right:** *Odm. gloriosum* is one of the high-elevation, cool-growing odonts. This species requires uniformly cool—50°Fahrenheit (10°Celsius) nights and 70°Fahrenheit (21°Celsius) days—and evenly moist conditions to do well. The 3" (8 cms) blooms are profusely borne on branching inflorescences, occasionally two to a growth. Plants are typically sized for this type, to 20" (51 cms) or, under best conditions, 30" (76 cms). This makes a good cymbidium companion on the West Coast. Available from South-American vendors at orchid shows.

**Left:** *Comparettia macroplectron* is known as a twig epiphyte, and comes from the very fringes of the forest, where conditions are extreme. Fast-growing and short-lived, *Comp. macroplectron* is a beautiful dwarf species, often under 8" (20 cms), suited to intermediate conditions. Grow on a cork mount and water frequently, allowing to dry well between waterings.

**Left:** *Odm. wyattianum* is another of the cloud forest odonts. Found at slightly lower elevations, it is more tolerant of warmer conditions, although it will sulk when temperatures rise much above 80°Fahrenheit (27°Celsius). The bronze 3" (8 cms) blooms are offset by a veined lip. Seed-raised populations are occasionally available from specialist growers. Keep evenly moist.

**Right:** *Oda.* Ross Newman *is* an intergeneric combination of the dwarf red cochlioda and larger odonts. Very little of the cochlioda influence remains in this 3" (8 cms), brilliant yellow bloom. Requires cool—50°Fahrenheit (10°Celsius) nights and 70°Fahrenheit (21°Celsius) days—and humid conditions. Keep moist and in moderate shade. Odont hybrids thrive in the cool Pacific Northwest.

many others, simply because the plants naturally occur from sea level to high in the Andes and vary accordingly in their temperature requirements.

An ironic side issue to the potting preferences of these plants is the presence of a significant number of species that do not appreciate potting at all. There is a class of plants that inhabit the very fringes of the forest canopy, under very extreme conditions of alternating moist and dry conditions, whose roots are constantly exposed and may barely attach to their hosts. Known as "twig epiphytes," these are among the prettiest, as well as most frustrating, of the *Oncidium* group.

These often tiny plants grow very quickly from seed to take advantage of their marginal, usually transient, habitats. This quick growth means that some may flower in as little as a year from seed, as with *Psygmorchis* (formerly *Oncidium*) *pusilla*, which has even been known to flower in the flask at commercial nurseries.

This quick growth is mirrored by an often short life, especially in cultivation. Only the most experienced growers report success with maintaining these over any length of time. One of the best loved is *Comparettia macroplectron*, an extraordinarily lovely pink bloom borne on an arching stem. The plants appear to be almost succulent, similar to a miniature mule-ear oncidium. They must be grown on a mount, in shady cattleya-like conditions, and enjoyed for as long as the grower can sustain them.

Another of the more frustrating members of this group are the high-elevation plants, best characterized by *Odm. crispum* and its hybrids, *Odm. gloriosum* and *Odm. wyattianum*. From only a few basic species, nineteenth and

early twentieth-century breeders created an entire spectrum of showy hybrids, such as the pristine *Odontoglossum* hybrid of Don Pancho x Pescalo and the brilliant yellow *Odm*. Ross Newman.

Starting with the wild collected plants of *Odm. crispum*—albeit highly selected ones—Charlesworths of England developed their Premier line of polyploid *Odm. crispum*, examples of which still set the world standard for this species. *Odm. crispum* is also highly variable from the wild, with varying degrees of spotting and barring over the white background. Some attribute this to natural hybridization with closely related yellow species that inhabit nearby areas.

Between the natural variation of the species, hybridization with other odonts, and the addition of the dwarf, fire-engine red species *Cochlioda noezliana*, the

modern spectrum of colors from white through yellow to orange and red has been created. The frustrating aspect of this hybrid group is that it is generally difficult to cultivate outside of areas that resemble the high-elevation forests from which it originates. In the same way that growers in the northeast have difficulty emulating the tropical habitat of vandas, so growers in warm climate find it nearly impossible to keep the mild day and cool night temperatures, without which odonts simply will not thrive.

In addition to mild climates, odonts are also quite finicky about their water quality and will not grow good roots where water is alkaline or high in dissolved solids. Poor root growth and high temperatures prove to make this group almost insurmountable for growers in the desert southwest and similar areas. Breeders have attempted, with great success, to create hybrids with more warmth-

**Left:** The lovely *Odm. crispum* is the basis of all of our full-formed modern odonts. Highly variable, from pure white to boldly mottled with red, this is a higher-elevation, cool-growing orchid that is not easy to grow. Gardeners in the Pacific Northwest and the Northeast find that they do well with this plant and its hybrids when they can provide the good quality water it demands, along with moderate days and nights. Ample shade is a method of keeping temperatures in check. Plants stay modest in size, up to 24" (61 cms), with arching, occasionally branching flower stems with up to a dozen or so blooms of 4" (10 cms).

**Right:** *Dgmna.* Kramer Island 'Everglades' AM/AOS. This complex intergeneric hybrid has *Odontoglossum*, *Miltonia*, and *Brassia* background, giving it a great deal of warmth tolerance. Growers in the Gulf States find this a wonderful way to get the benefits of odonts. Grow like a cattleya, allowing to dry between waterings. The flowers are borne rather closely spaced on 18" (46 cms) stems. Plants stay under 24" (61 cms) at maturity. Nights in the 60s Fahrenheit (18–21°Celsius) and days in the 80s (27–32°Celsius) will suit well. This type is becoming more freely available in garden centers and retail outlets.

**Left:** *Milt.* Brasilia 'Everglades' HCC/AOS is an unusual and floriferous Brazilian *Miltonia* hybrid of great appeal. Everyone can grow this type, whether in a sunny window, garden room, or outdoors. Upright stems of eight or more golden bronze blooms are freely produced on compact, under 20" (51 cms), plants. Allow to dry between watering and fertilize moderately while in active growth. *Milt.* Brasilia is more likely to be seen in retail outlets as a potted plant.

**Right:** *Mtssa.* Jungle Cat 'African Queen' HCC/AOS is an exotic example of the warm-tolerant plants now becoming more commonly available. It is the result of breeding the spider orchid, *Brassia verrucosa*, with a hybrid Brazilian *Miltonia*. Plants are strong growing, to 24" (61 cms) or so, with arching stems of perfectly arranged spidery blooms in unusual tones. Flowers are long-lasting. Fertilize regularly while in active growth and allow to dry between waterings.

tolerance. This has resulted in the warmer growing genera, such as *Oncidium, Brassia,* and *Miltonia* to make a race of intergeneric hybrids such as *Odontocidium, Odontobrassia, Odontonia,* and many others. These are generally much better subjects for warm-area situations, although some research may be necessary to ascertain if the particular plant is sufficiently tolerant for your area.

There is also a wide range of species and hybrids quite well suited to more typical growing conditions. It is during fall that we see plants of the archetypal Dancing Lady type oncidiums, such as *Onc.* (*Nonamyre* x *enderianum*), many of which are derived from the Brazilian *Onc. varicosum*. The truly warm-growing odonts, based in Brazilian *Miltonia* and *Brassia* background, are at their best now. Exotic primary hybrids such as *Odontobrassia* Kenneth

Bivens and more complex intergenerics like Degarmoara Kramer Island are commonly seen, along with straight Brazilian *Miltonia* hybrids like *Milt. Brasilia.* Wildly exotic *Miltassias* give long-lasting displays, as in *Mtssa.* Jungle Cat.

Thankfully, most, if not all, of the plants that the average consumer is liable to encounter in retail outlets are of these warmer growing and more tolerant types. Almost all will do well under the moderate light and temperature conditions that most casual gardeners are able to furnish. Additionally, many growers in frost-free areas find that this type makes an excellent addition to the outdoor growing zone, giving ample rewards for relatively little care. Indeed, *Oncidium* species, such as *Onc. sphacelatum,* are among the showiest and easiest of all orchids for the outdoor garden.

# CATTLEYAS

Fall-blooming cattleyas are relatively common, augmented by a spillover from the late summer types. Fall is the traditional season of the lavender cattleya and is the time when *C. labiata* naturally blooms. Historically it is renowned as the first cattleya to truly capture the public's interest in the mid-nineteenth century.

Some of the late-summer types that may continue their blooming into fall include *C. whitei* and *Lc. schilleriana*, both very easy and adaptable orchids for the inexperienced grower. The Guatemalan species, *C. bowringiana*, is a true harbinger of fall, when its tall bifoliate pseudobulbs burst forth with heads of medium-size lavender blooms. *C. bowringiana* is too large for home growing, but those with greenhouses or subtropical gardens will find it and its

**Right:** *C. bowringiana* coerulea. This unusual color form typifies the term coerulea as it is the silvery color one associates with blue roses. A form of the well-known Guatemalan species, *C. bowringiana* coerulea is often shorter than the lavender form, growing to 24" (61 cms). Heads of a dozen or more well-spaced 3" (8 cms) blooms appear in September. Copious water and fertilizer during growth will help to optimize flowering. Specialist nurseries may occasionally have this plant, but it remains rather rare and expensive.

**Left:** *C. whitei* coerulea is the blue form of a hybrid first registered in 1856. It is compact, growing to only 12" (30 cms) or so, and flowers from newly ripened growth in September. Mature examples will give two to four 5" (13 cms) blooms with hard substance and good lasting quality. A second flush of growth may emerge in late fall but may not flower. This type is often available from specialist growers who frequent orchid show sales.

**Left:** *Lc.* Hybrida coerulea. Sharing a parent with *C. whitei* (*C. warneri*), this is another remake of an early hybrid first registered in 1902. Because of its *L. pumila* parent, this plant will stay very compact, to no more than 10" (25 cms), and will have two or three blooms from newly ripening growth. It is a good garden plant in frost-free areas.

**Above left:** *Pot.* Sweet Cherry. *Slc.* Precious Stones, one of the parents of this rich red miniature, is famous for the quality and uniformity of its progeny. These plants will be of manageable size, 12" (30 cms) or less, and are perfect for home growing. Expect two to five 3–4" (8–10 cms) blooms in October. Can last to more than four weeks under favorable conditions.

**Above:** *Lctna.* Roy Fields 'Caesar's Creek' AM/AOS. One of the first of the complex *Bro. sanguinea* hybrids, *Lctna.* Roy Fields is an easy plant to grow. Plants remain under 15" (38 cms), and have strong, upright stems of four to eight or more 3" (8 cms) blooms with exceptionally rich color. Growers in south Florida find that it thrives well as a patio plant.

hybrids, such as *C. Portia*, worth searching out as grand display plants.

As the fall season progresses, more exotically colored blooms begin to be seen, including the *Broughtonia*-influenced *Lctna.* Roy Fields and the brilliantly colored *Pot.* Sweet Cherry, with strong red influence on both sides of its parentage. Both of these are quite compact, as well, making them very attractive as potted plants for indoor

use. Bifoliate influences are heavy in the spotted C. Mark Jones, exemplary of a type gaining much public acceptance.

Some favorite old-timers also show their blooms during the fall, such as *Sc.* Calypso, first registered in 1890 by the pioneering firm of Vietch. Such antique clones, also represented by the blue or coerulea *Lc.* Hybrida, not only retain their beauty, but add interest to a collection when it comes to conversation pieces.

One also must consider that plants remaining in cultivation over such a long period of time have special qualities worth searching out. The fall cattleya season is rounded out by a couple of fine species, *B. cordata*, with growth similar to its famous cousin, *B. nodosa*, and *Soph.* *cernua*, whose bright red-orange blooms are long lasting and do not require the uniformly cool temperature of its temperamental relatives. *Soph. cernua* makes an excellent mounted subject, and the clusters of blooms highlight the fascinating dwarf growth habit.

Another Brazilian species making its mark in this season is *L. gloedeniana*, closely related to the similar *L. flava*, with tall stems of golden yellow stars. This is an easy plant for high-light conditions, and will often do well as a cymbidium companion. Also blooming in fall, and another satisfactory subject for frost-free gardens, is *Enc. vitellina*, from higher elevations in Mexico. *Enc. vitellina* may prove to be difficult in warmer climates, but where conditions are right – cool nights and moderate days, mimicking the even temperatures of the mountain habitat – there is no more beautiful member of the genus.

**Left:** *L. gloedemana* (formerly known as a variety of *L. flava*), is typical of the Brazilian rupicolous, or rock-dwelling, laelias. Growing in strong light at middle elevations, the tall, strong flower stems have six to ten or more starry 2" (5 cms) yellow blooms. This is one of the easiest of this group to grow, provided a well-drained medium is used and pots are kept small. Plants should be kept on the dry side during winter months. *L. gloedeniana* and *L. flava* have made significant contributions to breeding very showy hybrids.

**Right:** *Enc. vitellina* is a beautiful species from higher elevations in the Mexican Sierra Madre mountains. Unfortunately, it is not the easiest to grow. Best results are attained where warm days and cool nights predominate, as on the Pacific Coast. The 1" (2.5 cms) blooms have an exceptionally rich orange color. Plants are dwarf, with upright leaves that may reach 12" (30 cms). Flower stems are upright, with blooms that open successively, carrying perhaps six open at any one time.

# VANDACEOUS ORCHIDS

The last of the year's vandaceous plants are also finishing up during the fall months. *Ascda.* Boris is a modern ascocenda that has all the appearances of its vanda heritage and very little of the ascocentrum, despite its compact stature. *Chtra.* Luang Prabang makes the most of the aerides background with tall, upright stems of many well-spaced blooms in an attractive combination of cream and pink. This is another very compact grower for the type. Vandaceous growth winds down during fall months, and growers should prepare for the cool months, when it is important to take advantage of the reserves stored during the final decent growing time that comes in fall.

**Left:** *Chtra.* Luang Prabang 'Elly's Passion Velvet' AM/AOS is a complex intergeneric hybrid that performs best in warmer climates with abundant sunshine and humidity. Plants are often as broad as tall, to 24" (61 cms) or so, and give upright foxtails of 2" (5 cms) pastel blooms, often accompanied by an enchanting fragrance.

**Above:** *Ascda.* Boris 'Iron Boy' AM/AOS. Highly bred, ascocendas have been called "Vandacendas" because they may contain so little of the ascocentrum influence. This flower certainly looks more like a vanda, and is of comparable size, over 30" (76 cms) tall. The rich yellow blooms approach 4" (10 cms). Suits warm vanda conditions.

# PHALAENOPSIS

Phalaenopsis are sparsely represented in fall months, unless they are remnants of summer bloomers or have been controlled for the season at a commercial facility. There are alternatives for those who *must* have phals in flower during this season. One is *Asconopsis* Irene Dobkin—though it is half *Ascocentrum* and extremely difficult to grow. Another, *Doritis pulcherrima* is an excellent choice. The small-growing plants produce a wealth of upright stems in a variety of colors ranging from the typical dark rose colors through white, peloric, or three lipped, to a cyanotic blue, or coerulea, form. Standard phals have grown well during the summer months, and the cool fall nights will trigger the season's inflorescences.

**Right:** *Asconopsis* Irene Dobkin is a compact plant that will need patience before it flowers. Because the plant is a cross between *Ascocentrum*, which needs high light, and *Phalaenopsis*, which is happy in lower light, it will need more light than ordinary phals.

**Right:** *Doritis pulcherrima* is available in a wide variety of colors. It has been used extensively in breeding with *Phalaenopsis* to produce *Doritaenopsis*. Doritis has a long flowering season and enjoys the same culture as *Phalaenopsis*. It can handle higher light and less water if adapted slowly.

# CYMBIDIUMS

The earliest cymbidiums begin to be seen toward the end of fall, especially those with higher warmth tolerance, which enables them to set spikes during warm months. Color range tends to be more limited in the early season cyms, with yellow and green being especially predominant. This is no bad thing with the newest hybrids, as with *Cym.* Milton Carpenter, a very bright yellow offset by a boldly banded lip. Flower life improves as the season progresses, with only a few weeks to be expected early in the fall, extending to a more normal four to six weeks in November. Most cymbidiums are just setting spikes during the early fall and will not be in bloom until January or February at the earliest.

**Left:** *Cymbidium* Bungy Jumper 'New Horizon'. The result of a cross between *Cym. canaliculatum* and *Cym. dayanum*, the single blooms branch off a central stem, producing an impressive spike of color.

**Above:** *Cym*. Milton Carpenter. These warm-tolerant plants display yellow 3–4" (8–10 cms) flowers with red spotted lips.

# SLIPPER ORCHIDS

Paphiopedilums again begin to show signs of flowering, after a summer lull. Now is when the Bulldog types first show their sheaths, giving promise of gaudy winter bloom. Maudiaes, which flower throughout the year, have a good flush of blooming—as in *Paph*. Fair Maud x *sukhakulii*—a rich amber green. Indeed, the lucky searcher may even come across an actual plant of the green *Paph*. Maudiae, which continues to be a standard against which other paphs are measured. Long-lived flowers ensure that these may bloom well into the Christmas season.

Some of the earliest of the multiflora types are also showing during fall, as demonstrated by *Paph*. Mirabel, which will have a semi-sequential, and hence long-lasting, floral display owing to the *Paph. chamberlainianum* in the background.

---

**Left:** *Paph*. Maudiae is arguably the best houseplant slipper ever. First registered in 1900, this hybrid has been remade countless times since, including green, red, and vinicolor (wine colored) forms. The green hybrid performs admirably in a home setting, preferring lower light and moderate temperatures. They respond well to occasional light feedings and repotting at just about any time of year. The foliage is marbled silver over green, with 4" (10 cms) flowers proudly held on 12" (30 cms) stems. The blooms can last to over six weeks or more.

---

**Right:** *Paph*. Lady Mirabel 'Krull Smith' AM/AOS. Multiflora strap leaf slippers are becoming increasingly popular. These are generally larger than most slippers, with foliage that may reach 30" (76 cms) across or more, and are slower to mature, often taking two to three years for a new growth to reach flowering size. Best results are achieved in a sunny window where they may be watered and fertilized copiously during the warmer months. Two to four flowers come in the fall on tall, up to 24" (61 cms), stems and are more than 6" (15 cms) across. Plants reluctant to flower may be coaxed into bloom by withholding fertilizer in the fall until buds show in the heart of the mature growth.

# DENDROBIUMS

Phalaenopsis-type dendrobiums, or "den phals," are available year-round and begin a seasonal peak during fall months. Originally only available in shades of lavender and white, breeders have extended the color range considerably, even to the inclusion of striped varieties like *Den.* Burana Stripe, a very fine example of the most modern breeding. Some of the longest lasting of all orchid flowers are in this genus.

Lovers of white blooms need look no further than *Den. longicornu*. This plant is closely related to *Den. formosum* in the group known as Nigrohirsutae—so called for the black hairs profusely borne on the pseudobulbs. A wealth of crystalline white blooms marked by bold yellow-throated lips may last for more than two months in perfection. The specific name, *longicornu*, refers to the prominent funnel shaped lip. This species comes from middle elevations of the Himalayan region of Nepal and Sikkim, thus may do well with a cool rest in winter months to encourage flowering.

Probably the longest lasting of the dendrobiums is the high-elevation species, *Den. cuthbertsonii*, from Papua New Guinea. Where conditions are conducive, as in the Pacific Northwest, great specimen plants of this small species often grow. They may produce a colorful array of blooms, lasting in excess of three months. Breeders have been quite active in extending the color range of this species beyond its typical cerise and into oranges, red, and even candy-corn two-tones. Uniformly cool and moist conditions are a must for success with this demanding, yet rewarding, species.

---

**Right:** *Den. longicornu* is one of the smaller growing, 6–12" (15–30 cms), of the Nigrohirsute group of dendrobiums. Long-lasting, crystalline white blooms are borne in clusters from the upper nodes. Suits well-drained mix and cool-intermediate conditions.

---

**Far right:** *Den. cuthbertsonii* are dwarf plants, under 3" (8 cms), with jewel-like foliage and flowers that can last up to six months or more. They need cool—under 70° Fahrenheit (21° Celsius) days, 50° Fahrenheit (10° Celsius) nights—and moist conditions. Where conditions are perfect, large specimen plants may be grown in pans of sphagnum moss.

# OTHER FALL-FLOWERING ORCHIDS

As fall draws to an end and the long winter lies ahead, it is worth noting a few last unusual species that add character to a collection. Bulbophyllums are almost always strange in some way or another, but one of the most beautiful and freest flowering is *Cirrhopetalum* Elizabeth Ann. (*Cirrhopetalum* was split off from *Bulbophyllum* based, in part, on the umbrella-like arrangement of the blooms.) *Cirr.* Elizabeth Ann, because of its long rhizomes and dislike of potting, after which it may sulk for a year or two before flowering, does well in slatted teak baskets in a medium that allows long periods between potting. Shady cattleya conditions suit it well.

Another good hanging-basket subject is *Coelogyne massangeana*, whose cascading stems of soft brown blooms are highlighted by a dark brown-edged, heavily keeled lip. Again, shady cattleya-type conditions will encourage this species. Smaller growing species are also prevalent during the fall, especially in the *Pleurothallid* group, where specialists find great joy in peering up close at the tiny, cool growing *Pleurothallis pubescens*, which is perfect for the underlights grower.

While so many orchids are grown for their sheer beauty, some are grown because they are simply different from everything else. *Trigonidium egertonianum* is such an orchid, whose compact bulbs bear upright stems of single, triangular, and very bizarre blooms. A final note of serene beauty is added by *Cochleanthes amazonica* in the soft leaf group, whose single pendant blooms are dominated by the circular white lip striped in grape purple. This species has been brought to a high level of perfection by several generations of selective breeding. It is an excellent and attractive plant for the home or frost-free garden.

**Left:** *Pths. pubescens.* Pleurothallids are often less than 6" (15 cms) tall. They require little care beyond watering and fertilizing and often enjoy the lower light levels prevalent in the home. The range of flower shapes and colors is fantastic. The plant pictured here is less than 4" (10 cms) tall.

**Right:** *Cirr.* Elizabeth Ann 'Buckleberry' FCC/AOS has won many awards. It is perhaps the most satisfactory hybrid in this genus. Suits basket culture, where the plants can remain undisturbed for long periods. Keep evenly moist.

# FREQUENTLY ASKED QUESTIONS

*To get the most out of growing and collecting orchids it's important that a beginner asks lots of questions, and these are the answers to the most frequently asked.*

**My orchid has finished flowering. Where do I cut the spike?**

This is by far the most frequently asked question concerning orchids. Why? The enormous popularity of phalaenopsis, the ubiquitous moth orchid—the number one potted orchid in the world by far—which will branch and rebloom from old inflorescences, has given the general public the mistaken notion that cutting the spike at the "wrong place" will cause the plant to never flower again.

Most orchids flower in their appropriate season and that's that. The spent inflorescence can be cut back to the base—with a sterile cutting tool, of course. Phals, on the other hand, will branch from nodes—the slightly raised areas covered by remedial leaves or bracts, which are along the flowering stem below the first flower. If spikes on phalaenopsis are cut above the last node after

flowering is finished, they will often produce a branched infloresence from that spike the following year. It is important to remove this section, as the tip of the inflorescence may continue to elongate and will give off hormones that will inhibit the development of the side branches.

Some few other orchids may branch, including reedstem epidendrums—especially the newer, shorter types now entering the mass market—and equitant oncidiums, occasionally seen in Florida and the Gulf States, so-called for their fan-shaped growth habit. Otherwise, simply remove the old stem at the base. It is as simple as that.

**How much light is "enough" light?**

The short answer is: If your hand, placed between the light source (a window, a skylight or a specialized lighting

**Left:** If spikes on *Phalaenopsis* are cut above the last node after flowering is finished, they will often produce a branched inflorescence from that spike the following year.

**Right:** When to water and how much to water is dependant on so many different elements; season, variety of orchid, medium, type of pot and location, all need to be factored in. The quality of water is important to some orchids, too.

fixture) and the plant, makes a faint shadow, there is "enough" light. The longer answer is another question: "Enough" light for what kind of orchid?

In the home, almost all light is incidental; that is, it comes at an angle through a window. Such light has less energy than light from directly overhead, i.e. outside or in a greenhouse. While experienced and dedicated windowsill growers manage to succeed with an astonishing array of widely differing orchids, they are limited to what will easily succeed in the home. And this, of course, is the critical first step—proper plant selection.

Orchids that will grow well in the home are generally those originating in the lower parts of the forest, where less light falls. Good examples are phalaenopsis (moth orchids) and paphiopedilums (slipper orchids), both of which will do quite well in the light conditions described above.

Such conditions are generally found in east (best),

lightly shaded south (next best) or west exposures. Northern exposures will rarely give enough light to successfully flower orchids of any kind.

So, when you want to know if there is "enough" light, if there is "enough" for phals or paphs, others matching these conditions will also do quite well. If you are able to provide slightly brighter conditions than those noted above, you will be successful with a much greater range of orchids, including many oncidium types, smaller-growing cattleyas, neofinetia hybrids and perhaps even some of the smallest of the new vandaceous hybrids.

### How do I get my orchid to flower?

The short answer is that you do not "get" your orchid to flower. Rather, you provide the proper conditions to "let" it flower. Orchid plants flower as a matter of course, when conditions allow them to grow properly, i.e. sufficient light,

**Left:** An orchid showing the growth effects of a sustained period of over-watering.

First, it's best to do some initial research—whether on the Internet or by asking the grower from whom you purchased your plant—and you can find out whether the plant does best when allowed to dry out between waterings, or needs to be kept more constantly moist.

Next, there are a couple of basic techniques for determining the amount of water remaining (or not) in a given plant. Lift the pot from the growing surface. Is it relatively heavy, indicating an ample amount of remaining moisture, or is it light, indicating that it is dry? If you have been growing it on a wooden surface, is there a ring of moisture under the pot? A sharpened pencil is another useful tool. Insert the pencil into the growing medium a couple of inches and then withdraw it. If the exposed wood is dark with moisture, you have good moisture in the pot; if it is dry, so is the plant.

Perhaps the least preferable method, due to the different types of media in which orchids are commonly grown, is the probe-type water meter. The accepted opinion is that you are better off learning to judge for yourself.

Growing plants grouped by type and pot size is another aid to knowing when to water. Once you've grown your plants for a while, testing them using the above methods, you will develop an instinct for when certain types need water under changing circumstances.

## When do I repot?

It's best to repot every two years, in the spring. Almost all orchids are seasonal in their growth and rooting cycles, some if only to the extent that there are better or worse times. In general, orchids do the majority of their growing between the two equinoxes—the Vernal Equinox around March 21 and the Autumnal Equinox around September 21. Their growth spurt is triggered by day length, and, depending on how far from the Equator you are, will initiate roughly in late March or April.

The further north from the Equator you are, the later your growing season will begin. Potting is best undertaken early in the growing season, to allow plants maximum time to re-establish and grow prior to the colder, darker winter months. The further north one goes, the more critical this becomes, as the effectiveness of the shorter

water, nutrients and temperature. Only very rarely will an orchid require a "trick" to flower it, and these are not suitable for novice growers in any case. Obstinate orchids are not only reluctant to flower, they will be more rarely grown by commercial horticulturalists who can't be bothered with a plant that is an unpredictable bloomer, and hence they are more expensive. Some of the showier bulbophyllums are good examples of this, such as *Bulbo. rothschildianum* or *Bulbo. phalaenopsis*.

## When do I water?

The short answer is, when they need it. But how do you know when the plant needs water?

growing season must be maximized. As illustrated elsewhere in this book, it is also important to learn to recognize when, during the growth cycle of any particular orchid, rooting initiates. For example, if you have observed—and keen observation is the key to successful orchid culture—that a given plant initiates its roots in the late spring when its new growth is about halfway to its mature size, this is the time to repot.

Yes, it is good to actually observe new roots emerging, but if you know that they will be coming at a certain growth stage, it is far preferable to pot just prior to this stage, as damage to the emerging root tips is much less likely in this case.

Another issue to be aware of is the lifespan of the medium you find best for your conditions. Orchid mix, unless it is an inert medium such as Aliflor or Diatomite, breaks down under the action of nutrients and moisture. Firbark-based media are particularly susceptible to breakdown, as the lasting quality of firbark has decreased over the past ten years or so.

Generally, for most of your plants, potting every two years is the norm, even when the medium clearly lasts longer. However, it is okay to be mean with space, as it is not advisable to overpot orchids for many reasons.

### How do I choose the right mix?

There are two factors to consider in this question, the right mix for the orchid, and the right mix for the grower, based on his particular conditions, as well as the area in which he lives.

There are five factors that go into making a good orchid mix:

- Readily available
- Easily reproduced
- Cost-effective
- Long-lasting
- Effective for the orchid

All of the above need to be taken into account, whether you choose to make your own mix from ingredients purchased from local suppliers, or you simply use what is made available at the local garden center or warehouse

---

**Below:** A clear case of an orchid that has been left to its own devices for too long, in desperate need of repotting.

Left: If you can easily pull away the spongy velamen covering from a root, revealing the wiry inside, the root can be removed.

store. A good tip when considering premade mixes is to look at the bottom of the bag. If there is a significant amount of dusty fine material in the bottom it is a good bet that the manufacturer is careless with their procedures.

You will also need to take into account what is locally appropriate and in use. The retailer will stock what is most commonly available from his suppliers, not necessarily what is best for your orchids. A good place to start in your investigations as to what works in your area is a visit to your local orchid society's monthly meeting. You can visit and talk with the members, as well as observe what they use to grow their orchids. The best-grown orchids will almost always be from one or a few of the members, and their mix choice should be yours.

In general, however, more finely-rooted orchids require finer, more water-retentive media; while orchids with thicker, fleshier, roots prefer a coarser, well-drained mix.

### I get nervous about cutting off roots. Is there any way to easily tell dead roots from live?

With experience you will be able to tell good roots from bad at a glance. Although it varies from genera to genera,

dead roots are soft and mushy while live roots are firm. Dead roots are often brown, but this is not a reliable indicator for all genera as there are some orchids whose roots are normally brown.

A useful test is to pinch a root between thumb and forefinger and pull away from the plant. If you can easily pull away the spongy velamen covering from a root revealing the wiry inside, the root can be removed. We are not suggesting that you test every root, but this can give you a clue about a particular orchid. If you follow the suggestion of repotting only when there is active new root growth, knowing which roots to cut is not as critical.

### Which are better, clay or plastic pots?

Like many factors of orchid culture, this depends on your growing location. Plastic pots will retain moisture for a longer period than clay pots. So if you are growing indoors or in a greenhouse and only have time to water your orchids once or twice a week, plastic pots are a good choice. They are also good in the home environment because the microclimate of a house is usually overly dry and lacking in humidity. If you are growing your orchids outdoors in a rainy subtropical area like Florida, clay pots are more suitable.

### Should paphiopedilums be grown in sphagnum and charcoal instead of bark?

There is no single solution for orchid culture. What works for one person may not work for another. It is wise to try a new culture technique on one or a few plants before committing your entire collection to it. If friends are having success with their paphs using sphagnum and charcoal, try a few potted in this medium. Evaluate the results over a full year's growth and subsequent flowering before moving all of your paphs into this mix. Every orchid grower has "secret recipes." The potting demonstrations will provide you with the basics on which to build your knowledge.

### When should I begin watering a repotted orchid?

There are two schools of thought on this matter. Some say that you should withhold water for a week or two (until roots are active), suggesting that drier conditions will encourage roots to seek moisture. They advocate only misting plants during this period. We tend to favor the other school of thought, which is to water repotted orchids normally, along with your other orchids. We feel that repotting an orchid, no matter how careful you are, causes stress to the plant. The humidity created by moist potting media will help ease the stress. If you have potted the orchid at the right time there should be root growth already.

### Where is the best place to buy an orchid?

While many people receive their first orchid plant as a gift, others actively seek out their first plant. The short answer here is anywhere you see an orchid that you might like to enjoy—and where the plants seem to be in good health and reasonably priced—is an acceptable place.

With orchid plants, one of the aspects for which you may choose to pay a bit of a premium is expertise. The more unlikely the venue for orchid sales, the less chance there is that the seller can offer quality advice. If you already know what you're doing, and know the plant, this is not a drawback, and some exceptional bargains can be found in this way.

However, if you are new to orchids, you may wish to go to a garden center for your orchid needs, as the nursery professionals there are more likely to be able to offer quality advice as to how to grow the plant in question. In some cases, you may simply want to purchase a favorably priced plant in the knowledge that you will only be able to enjoy it as long as it is in flower, then discard.

This concept is anathema to traditional orchid hobbyists, but with so many plants entering the market today the majority is destined for this fate.

Also, many of today's mass-produced plants are grown so quickly, under such perfect conditions, that they inevitably suffer when placed in less-than-ideal circumstances. This is not necessarily bad, just another factor to be aware of. A mass-produced orchid plant may take longer to acclimatize to your local conditions than one produced by a nearby grower.

Things to look for in an orchid plant that you intend to purchase are:

- Is it steady in the pot? If it "rocks," it may not be well established and therefore have flowers that last poorly, or the plant may be more difficult to grow to flowering in following years.
- Are their flower buds to come on the flowering stem? If not, you cannot know how long the flowers have been open prior to your purchase, so you cannot know how much longer you can expect them to last. If so, you can be reasonably assured that the flowers are relatively fresh and will last their best.
- Is the general appearance of the plant and flowers fresh and healthy or run down and disheveled? If a plant has been poorly handled—whether in transit to the selling point, by the seller, or by a careless grower —it will perform poorly.

### My orchid is in flower; do I need to fertilize it?

In short, yes. At perhaps no other time in the growth cycle of an orchid are more of its resources and reserves in active use than when the plant is producing and supporting flowers. Clearly, such large, colorful, and fragrant blooms take considerable energy to grow and maintain. Indeed, some orchid flowers are so complex and energy depleting that the blooms only last a very short time, in some cases a day or less.

In other cases, of course, orchid blooms are among the longest lasting of all flowers. If, for example, a paphiopedilum or cymbidium were to be deprived of

fertilizer-supplied nutrients during the many weeks the flowers can last, it would represent a severe loss to the plant even if it were not in flower.

So, yes, fertilize at your normal rate and frequency during flowering. If you find that the plant is using more water, by drying more quickly than expected, you might find it advantageous to increase the fertilizer a bit, too.

### What kind of fertilizer should I use?

The answer to this one begins with a question. What medium are you using for your plants? The type of mix you are using determines the type of fertilizer you should be using for best results. Firbark-based media require a fertilizer proportionately high in nitrogen to offset the nitrogen used by the organisms that break down the bark. For most other commonly-used media, a balanced formula is indicated.

How can you tell how a fertilizer is formulated? Read the label. A bit of label reading will result in better plants. You will always see a formula such as 10-10-10, or 30-10-

**Above:** Healthy phalaenopsis plants in a commercial nursery in southern Florida start to send up flower spikes.

10, or 0-5-10. This represents the N-P-K formula, or the amounts of available nitrogen (N), phosphorous (P), and potassium (K).

Nitrogen is necessary for plant growth, while phosphorous and potassium are for roots and flowers. Firbark-appropriate fertilizers are usually seen as 30-10-10, or 20-10-10, to provide the greater amount of nitrogen needed. A balanced fertilizer will appear as 10-10-10 or 5-5-5. Another factor to consider is the source for the nitrogen. Generally, urea-derived nitrogen is less available and less desirable than that derived from ammoniacal sources. This is a cost-driven decision on the part of the manufacturer, as urea-based nitrogen is cheaper and more stable than ammoniacal. However, urea-based nitrogen requires the action of soil bacteria to become available to the plant.

# GLOSSARY

**aerial root:** Any root produced above the growing medium.

**anther:** The part of the stamen containing the pollen; the end of the column.

**back bulbs:** Old pseudobulbs behind the part of a sympodial orchid that is actively growing. Although there may be no leaves the presence of undamaged "eyes" is a sign that growth is possible.

**bifoliate:** Having two leaves.

**cane:** An elongated pseudobulb, usually used when describing dendrobiums.

**crock:** Small pieces of broken earthenware or flower pots, placed in the bottom of a pot. Aids drainage when repotting.

**cultivar:** An individual plant and its vegetative propagations in cultivation; a horticultural variety.

**epiphyte, epiphytic:** A plant which naturally grows upon another plant but does not derive any nourishment from it. Many of the orchids in cultivation are epiphytic in the wild.

**eye:** The bud of a sympodial orchid that will eventually develop into a new lead.

**foliar spray:** Many minor nutrients and trace elements beneficial to growth are best absorbed through the stomata of orchids leaves when mixed with water and sprayed on the plant.

**genus:** (pl. genera) A natural grouping of closely related species.

**habitat:** The type of place in which a plant normally grows.

**hybrid:** The offspring of a cross between species or hybrids.

**inflorescence:** The flowering portion of a plant.

**intergeneric hybrid:** A hybrid between members of two or more genera.

**keiki:** A Hawaiian word referring to a baby plant produced asexually by an orchid plant, usually used when referring to dendrobiums or vandaceous orchids.

**lead:** An immature vegetative growth on a sympodial orchid that will develop into a flower-producing structure.

**lip:** A modified petal of the orchid flower specialized to aid in pollination and different than the other petals.

**lithophyte:** An orchid that grows on rocks.

**medium:** The material in which an orchid is container-grown; it may be organic such as firbark or inorganic such as lava rock.

**mericlone:** A plant derived from tissue culture that is identical to its parent.

**monopodial:** Orchids that grow upward from a single stem, producing leaves and flowers along that stem.

**node:** A joint on a stem or pseudobulb from which a leaf or growth originates.

**panicle:** An inflorescence with a main stem and branches; the flowers on the lower branches open earlier than the upper ones.

**photosynthesis:** The process a plant uses to produce carbohydrates and sugar from water and carbon dioxide in the air using chlorophyl-containing cells exposed to light.

**pseudobulb:** A thickened portion of the stem of many orchids functioning as a water and food storage device.

**raceme:** An unbranched inflorescence of stalked flowers.

**rhizome:** A root-bearing stem of sympodial orchids that progressively sends up leafy shoots.

**scape:** An unbranched inflorescence with one flower.

**sheath:** A modified leaf that encloses an emerging inflorescence or leaf.

**species:** A kind of plant that is distinct from other plants.

**spike:** An unbranched inflorescence of unstalked flowers.

**stolon:** A branch that grows horizontally above the medium and produces roots and shoots at the nodes.

**stomata:** The breathing pores on the surface of a plant's leaves.

**sympodial:** Orchids that grow laterally and produce leafy growths along a rhizome.

**terrestrial:** Growing on the ground and supported by soil.

**unifoliate:** Having one leaf.

**velamen:** The thick sponge-like covering of the roots of epiphytic orchids that helps prevent water loss and aids in absorption.

**virus:** A type of infectious agent, much smaller than common microorganisms, several forms of which affect certain kinds of orchids.

# INDEX

# BIBLIOGRAPHY & ACKNOWLEDGMENTS

## Bibliography

*American Cattleyas*, Courtney T. Hackney (Self published, 2004)

*The Cattleyas and Their Relatives: V.I The Cattleyas*, Carl A. Withner (Timber Press, Portland, Oregon, 1988)

*The Cattleyas and Their Relatives: V.III Schomburgkia, Sophronitis and Other South American Genera*, Carl A. Withner (Timber Press, Portland, Oregon, 1993)

*The Cattleyas and Their Relatives: V.V Brassavola, Encyclia and Other Genera of Mexico and Central America*, Carl A. Withner (Timber Press, Portland, Oregon, 1998)

*Encyclopedia of Cultivated Orchids*, Alex D. Hawkes (Faber and Faber, London, 1965)

*Genera Orchidacearum V.I*, Pridgeon, Cribb, Chase and Rasmussen (Oxford University Press, Oxford, England, 1999)

*A History of the Orchid*, Merle A. Reinikka (Timber Press, Portland, Oregon, 1995; first published in 1972)

*Orchids and Their Conservation*, Harold Koopowitz (Timber Press, Portland, Oregon, 2001)

*The Orchids: A Scientific Survey*, Carl L. Withner (The Ronald Press Company, New York, 1959)

*The Orchids: Natural History and Classification*, Robert L. Dressler (Harvard University Press, Cambridge, Massachusetts and London, England, 1981)

*Orchid Species Culture: Dendrobium*, Margaret L. and Charles O. Baker (Timber Press, Portland, Oregon, 1996)

*The Paphiopedilum Grower's Manual*, Lance A. Birk (Pisang Press, Santa Barbara, California, 1983)

*Phalaenopsis: A Monograph*, Eric A. Christenson (Timber Press, Portland, Oregon, 2001)

*Phylogeny and Classification of the Orchid Family*, Robert L. Dressler (Dioscorides Press, Portland, Oregon, 1993)

*Vandas and Ascocendas and their Combinations with Other Genera*, David L. Grove (Timber Press, Portland, Oregon, 1995)

## Acknowledgments

**Ned Nash:** Without the help and support of my wife, Debra, I wouldn't have been able to produce this work. But even more profoundly influential were the many old-school orchid people who kindly shared their hard-won experience and information with me. Chief amongst them is my mentor and best teacher, Leo Holguin, who, along with his recently and sadly departed wife, Irene, taught me how to be not just an orchid man, but a man.

**Greg Allikas:** One cannot take superlative orchid portraits of mediocre orchids. I would like to thank all of the exhibitors in Florida and abroad who have brought their best orchids to AOS judging events, and congratulate them on their many awards and considerable orchid growing skills. Without such a steady stream of high standard orchids my photo archive would be of far less quality. I would also like to thank Kathy for her unwavering support of my photographic endeavors and help with all associated tasks. Her encouragement has made my successes possible.

*Learn about orchids*
Join the American Orchid Society today:
16700 AOS Lane
Delray Beach, FL 33446
www.aos.org